Breaking the Mould

Prose Series 37

Penny Petrone

Breaking the Mould

*To Charles Wilkins,
my warmest wishes
Penny Petrone*

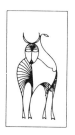

Guernica
Toronto / New York
1995

Copyright © Penny Petrone and Guernica Editions Inc., 1995.
All rights reserved.

This publication was made possible in part with a grant from
Canadian Heritage (Multiculturalism), The Ontario Arts Council
and The Canada Council.

Antonio D'Alfonso, Editor.
Guernica Editions Inc.
P.O. Box 117, Station P, Toronto (Ontario), Canada M5S 2S6
340 Nagel Drive, Cheektowaga, N.Y. 14225-4731 U.S.A.

Legal Deposit — Second Quarter
National Library of Canada
Library of Congress Catalog Card Number: 94-77150

Canadian Cataloguing in Publication Data

Petrone, Penny
Breaking the mould: a memoir

(Prose series; 37)
ISBN 1-55071-033-8

1. Petrone, Penny — Biography. 2. Authors, Canadian
(English) — 20th century — Biography. I. Title. II. Series.

PS8025.P48A3 1995C818'.5409C94-900810-9
PR9183.P48A3 1995

Table of Contents

1. The Myth of America 7
2. Port Arthur 17
3. Mamma 41
4. Daddy 77
5. The Neighbourhood 97
6. Italo-Canadese 121
7. Food 127
8. Religion 147
9. School Days: Cornwall and
   St. Joseph's 165
10. Port Arthur Collegiate Institute . . . 179
11. War Years 193
12. Epilogue 223
13. Acknowledgements 229
14. List of Photographs 231

Dedicated to Lisa, Krista, Sandy, Jana, Alicia, Elysia, Ryan, Kyle, Jessica, Brittney and Cody; and in loving memory of Luigi and Luisa Petrone

1
The Myth of America

There was great rejoicing in the home of Luigi and Luisa Petrone on the day that I was born. It was a long awaited arrival. In fact, Daddy had begun to despair that Mamma was barren. But after two years of marriage with the special intercession of the Saints, and the help of a midwife, she delivered in her big brass bed.

I was named Serafina and affectionately called Serafinella. Daddy named me after his mother, and there were no other names given me. Eventually I rejected the name. I should have been honoured by it. My paternal grandmother, whom I never knew, was as formidable as the rugged terrain of the Calabrian mountains that gave her birth. Wiry and vigorous, Serafina could work all day "like a man." In pantaloons and on horseback she rode great distances overseeing the family's grazing cattle, goats and flock of sheep, three hundred strong.

She governed her life by the ancient poetry of the Calabrian peasants: *Chine lassa la via vecchia e va la nova/ Sa chi lassa/ Ma un sa chi trova* (Whoever leaves the old road for the new knows what he is losing but not what he will find). And yet, in her day, thousands of young Calabrese did leave the old road — mostly for America.

For, at the turn of the century, in impoverished Southern Italy, it was said that America was a paradise where everyone was rich and the streets were paved with gold. So seductive was this myth that little Calabresi boys came to worship *gli Americani*, the young men who returned from America to visit or stay in their remote hometowns. "*Mamma dammi 100 lire*," they sang, "*perché in America voglio andar*" (Mamma, give me 100 lire, because I want to go to America).

In their showy American clothes — high-buttoned shoes, derbies, celluloid collars, blue serge suits, flashy neckties and gold watches — *gli Americani* cut fine figures as they strutted about smoking Havana cigars, visiting relatives, distributing presents. They told fantastic tales of the bountiful continent.

For the little Calabresi boys who followed them wherever they went, *gli Americani* were heroes, like their countryman, the great Cristoforo Colombo, who nearly five centuries before, had been the first to conquer the seas and reveal the presence of the New World to unsuspecting Europeans in the name of God and the Queen of Castile. Like Colombo, they had overcome a host of preliminary obstacles — from getting the necessary funds, passports, pictures, and steamship tickets to contending with the government bureaucracy for legal papers. And the journey itself must have been just as intimidating as that first voyage was to Colombo. For these young men were rooted in the static and staid culture of the *Mezzogiorno* mountains, where peasants were born and died in the same house. Yet, venture they did, *gli Americani*, in numbers unparalleled in the annals of Western immigration.

My father, Luigi Antonio Petrone, son of Serafina Covello and Leonardo Petrone was one of those little Calabresi boys whose imagination was stirred with promises of excitement and unimaginable treasures. His mountain town, Aprigliano, perched on the top of a steep cliff, where, like many towns in Calabria, it had been built in ancient times to protect its inhabitants against invaders, brigands, and the malaria that infected the marshy lowlands. From the age of six, when he started to tend the family's flock of sheep, he had dreamed of the distant wonder-world.

In 1900, when he was eleven, his dream came true. With money his grandmother gave him, the little shepherd boy departed for America, in the company of a guardian whose identity has been lost. As extraordinary as this seems, it was not uncommon in Calabria for boys as young as Luigi to be taken to the fabled land. From our late twentieth century perspective, it is difficult to comprehend that either children or parents could have tolerated such separation. Unfortunately, no information is available about my father's departure beyond the fact itself. He never spoke about it.

When Luigi arrived in the wilds of Northern Ontario, his guardian sent him to school in

North Bay. He was the oldest and biggest boy in the primer class. He spoke no English and wore knee breeches. The other children made fun of him, and he got into a fight. The principal threatened him with expulsion if the incident reoccurred. It did.

After only a week at school, Luigino, as he was affectionately called, quit. He was thrust into Canada's migrant labour force where he remained for the next ten years.

Nothing more is known about this period of Luigi's life. In 1910 he returned to Calabria for his military service. He served with the 9th Infantry Brigade during the Libyan War of 1911-12, in which the Italians took Tripoli from the Turks. He received an honourable discharge on December 1, 1911, a month after his father had died of bronchial pneumonia.

The widow Serafina fully expected Luigi to settle into the family's expanding business endeavours. Although cash was scarce, the farm was beginning to flourish. It was the first in the Marchesato-Crotonese region to use agricultural machinery.

But the restless bachelor was determined to return to North America, even though he knew, first-hand, that Canada was not the promised land with golden streets.

Even as Luigi was departing, Serafina wept and wailed. She made a last desperate attempt to pull him from the steps of the train. To the horror of the bystanders, she fell backwards on the station platform. But with overwhelming singlemindedness, her son entered the train car and remained there.

His assault on parental authority, one of the cornerstones of the centuries-old Calabrian peasant-feudal culture, was seen as a glaring example of the New World's disastrous influence. To defy a mother's pleas and wilfully abandon one's family, in a society where long years of regional isolation made the family sacrosanct, simply wasn't done. His mother and family were horrified.

Luigi sailed from Naples on the Duca di Genova on September 18, 1912, for New York. He travelled steerage, sleeping in the bowels of the ship where hundreds, perhaps even a thousand or more, were squeezed into cramped quarters breathing stifling air. The stench of vomit, urine and excrement, as well as the moans and wails of the seasick, must have made the thirteen-day crossing a nightmare.

On October 1, Luigi arrived in New York with his papers in order. The next day he crossed the Canadian border at Athelstan, Quebec, and headed for Port Arthur.

Eight years later, my mother, Luisa Sisco, daughter of Saverio Sisco and Agata Mauro from Piane Crati, twelve kilometres down the mountainside from Aprigliano, had departed for Port Arthur with her mother, a sister and brother. She was twenty-three years old. Her beloved father, whom she always called *Tata*, had died three years earlier, and her older brother, Pasquale, whom she adored, had been beaten to death soon after, at the age of twenty-four.

As tradition decreed, the fatherless family fell under the guidance of the sons, three of whom were already in North America: Giovanni and Giustino in Port Arthur and Pietro in Chicago.

The Siscos, like the Petrones, were respected *contadini* (land-owning peasants). Although they did not own animals, their land produced enough crops for their own use and some to sell. They were comfortable.

Under the terms of his will, Saverio had bequeathed to all his children, boys and girls, equal parts of his estate. He asked them "to love each other and to respect and venerate their mother." He also bequeathed to his beloved wife an extra portion of the estate if she remained a widow.

My mother and grandmother — plus my mother's older sister Maria and younger brother Ciccilu — deliberated for three years before they reluctantly decided to join the rest of the family. The Calabrese proverb — *Tutto il mondo è paese* (The world is one village) — a notion that would be popularized by Marshall McLuhan — reassured them. Besides, it was *la volontà di Dio* (God's will). It was their destiny. The Calabrese perceive *il destino* as the underpinning of life itself. To deny this awful force which predetermines the fate of mortals is to court disaster. It is part of the great design wrought by God just as surely as the seasons come and go. Their fate lay in America.

Only one anecdote survives from their long journey to Port Arthur. My mother, Luisa, saw her first black man at the Montreal railroad station and was frightened. However, a reassuring smile from the black porter assuaged her fears. His words — "It's alright, lady" — were riveted in her memory.

In Port Arthur, Luisa lived above her brother Giovanni's grocery store at 350 John Street. She set about earnestly to adapt to life in the New World. She knew about the physical hardships, the fierce winters and hard work. (Her Uncle Francesco who spent fourteen years in America had returned to Piane Crati, disillusioned, his back injured from years of swinging a pick.) But she was not prepared for the absence of social refinements of the sort she had been accustomed to. In the Old World, for instance, a high degree of courtly formality and respect existed for the dignity of woman. Over here, men did not even doff their hats to her as they had always done when they passed her in Piane Crati.

This affected her deeply. As did a conversation she had with her brother Giovanni shortly after her arrival. "Did you see Mr. — on Cumberland Street in front of Giustino's store a few days ago?" he asked.

"Yes," was Luisa's reply.

"Well, he told me that you were showing off your schooling and putting on airs speaking the high Italian. He reminded me that we were now living in America. So from now on, speak the peasant dialect — the coarser, the better."

A subsequent experience convinced her that she was going to have serious problems with English. When a Canadian friend of Giovanni's brought her baby to the store, Luisa asked her niece, Assunta, what to say to the infant. Assunta replied, "Say hello, nice baby," and added in exasperation, "Oh, I don't know." Luisa joined all the words together, "HellonicebabyohIdon'tknow." Everyone burst out laughing, and thereafter Assunta refused to be her Aunt's teacher.

Luisa had wanted to be a nun, but she was destined to be a wife. She had learned to spin and weave, sew, embroider, do fancy cutwork, cross-stitch, crochet, knit. She had brought with her to Canada a trunk containing her *corredo da cucina* (kitchen dowry) — hand-stitched tablecloths and napkins, linen hand towels with long strands of flax fringe — as well as her *corredo da letto* (bedroom dowry). The bedroom treasures consisted of hand-embroidered bedspreads and pillow shams, hand-monogrammed sheets and pillowcases, nightgowns and chemises with crocheted bodices and a queen-size *coperta matrimoniale* (marriage bedspread) crocheted to last forever. My favourite is still a large white sham bearing the hand-embroidered wish *Notte Felice* (A happy night). She brought with her, too, a mind stocked with the folk wisdom of Calabria.

2
Port Arthur

At the turn of the century when Luigi arrived in Northern Ontario, Port Arthur and Fort William were rough and ready frontier towns. Hacked out of the wilderness, they stood on the shores of the world's largest lake.

Fort William was the older of the two, having begun as a French fur-trading post in the late seventeenth century. Significant European presence began in the area during the nineteenth century when the fort became the inland headquarters of the North West Company's vast fur-trading empire.

Port Arthur traces its origins to 1858 when the North-West Transit Company established the location as a depot for its mailship *Rescue*. Real development began ten years later with the discovery of rich silver deposits at nearby Silver Islet and the construction of a road to the Red River followed by the arrival of the Red River Military Expedition under Colonel Garnet Wolseley.

The two cities were isolated and remained virtually unreachable until the 1880s when the determined General Manager of the CPR, William Van Horne, bucked the opinions of experts and built his railroad along the north shore of Lake Superior. With the arrival of the railroad and new trade in grain and timber, the Twin Cities became progressive urban centres. Port Arthur was soon running its own street railway, electric light, telephone and water systems. And a road was built across the four miles of bush and swamp that separated Port Arthur from Fort William. But a growing mutual hostility had already begun to mar the relationship between the two cities. According to local legend, when in 1888 Port Arthur's mayor tried to collect back taxes on the CPR's right of way and seized rolling stock as collateral, the CPR's Van Horne was incensed. He told the Mayor that he would live to see the grass growing on Port Arthur's main street. He chose Fort William as the CPR's Lakehead terminal point. Port Arthur was outraged. The hostility existed until 1970 when the Ontario Government mandated the amalgamation of the two cities. When I was growing up we called Fort William "Frog-town." They called us "Ant-hill."

Nevertheless, so great was the optimism for the two cities in 1905 that, when Sir Wilfred Laurier turned the first sod for the Grand Trunk Pacific Railway in Fort William, he predicted there would soon be a Chicago of the North on the shores of Lake Superior.

When Luigi arrived in 1912, Port Arthur's economy was booming. Its grain shipping and storage industries were developing rapidly, as were its manufacturing plants, timber operations and construction trade. The Gateway to the West, as Port Arthur was called, was a regular port-of-call for the S.S. Hamonic, S.S. Huronic and S.S. Saronic on their way to Duluth. The Noronic, the largest fresh water passenger steamer in the world, and the future flagship of the Canada Steamship Lines, was under construction at the Port Arthur Shipyards. The storage capacity of Port Arthur's grain elevators, already the greatest in the world, was being increased to meet the demand of the burgeoning shipments of prairie grain. Construction was underway on the tallest building in the Twin Cities, the magnificent eight-storey Whalen Building, which would complement splendid existing buildings, such as the Prince Arthur Hotel, the Lyceum Theatre and the Port Arthur Collegiate Institute. All of these were of course dwarfed by the massive elevators, which towered majestically, befitting the immensity and nobility of the world's largest body of fresh water.

Watching over the elevators at the entrance to the harbour stood Thunder Cape, an impressive rock formation, silhouetted in benign repose against the horizon. The Ojibwa called the cape Nanabijou, the Sleeping Giant, believing it a manifestation of the Great Spirit who had once lived on nearby Mount McKay.

The combined scenic effect of the stately elevators and the Sleeping Giant is unrivalled among industrial harbours. A few years ago the harbour lights and floodlit elevators caught the attention of my five year old great-niece, Jana, who when she saw them from my living room windows on a dark Halloween night exclaimed,

"Oh, look at the beautiful castles." She did not know that nearly a century earlier Rudyard Kipling had called them "castles of commerce."

Considering the port's strategic location, with its railroads, grain trade, water power possibilities, and adjacent resources of mineral and forest land, there was no doubt as to the future of Port Arthur. Not Van Horne's curse, but Laurier's prediction seemed well on its way to fulfilment. In 1900 the population was 2,779 and, in 1910, 15,000 — a phenomenal increase of 500%.

With so much work available, Luigi did not have difficulty finding a job. During his first stay in Canada, he had worked at a variety of construction jobs throughout Northern Ontario — Dryden, Rossport, Shabaqua and Chapleau. He had shovelled earth and carried water pails, had pushed wheelbarrows and swung a sledge hammer and pick. He had pounded cross-ties and lifted rails. He had dug ditches. During his mid-teens, he had become a powder man's helper, had learned how to use and store explosives and to blast rock. According to family lore, he was made foreman of a road gang at the age of fourteen. He was robust, square-shouldered and looked older than his years. He could keep discipline and settle quarrels within a gang of men.

Construction work in the North was fraught with problems: unpredictable weather, the danger of rock falls, landslides and precarious excavations. There was also the difficulty of having to work on the bottomless muskeg of the Canadian Shield. Employers trusted Luigi because he handled emergencies well. He was willing to go wherever the work took him. He was venturesome and adaptable, like the Orkney men preferred by the Hudson's Bay Company for work on isolated posts. Had not the lonely nights he spent as a youngster steeling himself against the darkness and the howling of wild animals as he watched his flocks of sheep, prepared him for this?

Once winter set in, Luigi, like all the migrant labourers, was laid off. He made his way to the Twin Cities.

Many Italians returned yearly to the Old Country, to their parents or families left behind in their *paese*. Or they went to find a bride and to father children. In 1906 one-third of Toronto's Italians went back to their hometowns for the winter. Those like Luigi who stayed in Port Arthur or Fort William congregated in a few overcrowded boarding houses where they spent the winter. The houseowner's wife cooked, cleaned and washed for them, taking on work that women never did in Calabria. The *bordanti* (boarders) tried to live as cheaply as they could to save money.

In the coal dock sections of the Twin Cities, it was not uncommon to find as many as thirteen Italians living in a house of three rooms. Kitchens and halls were used as dining and living rooms. A common bathroom served all. Bath tubs and indoor toilets were rare, water taps scarce, ventilation poor; the removal of garbage was inadequate.

An article in the January 10, 1914 issue of the *Daily News-Chronicle* recorded the comparison one Italian made between the coal docks and Mariday Park, the best residential area in Port Arthur:

> Thousands and thousands of dollars have been spent in Mariday Park, which has about one-third the people the coal dock has. T'at is verra good. It maka nica street, nica place to live, but we who live in de coal dock have not got near dat much and we are tree times as big as the peoples in Mariday Park.
>
> I know dat money is tight and de council will have hard time to get much, but we will be fair. We don't want what we can't get, but we would like some'ting done. It's alright if council only do lettle now, den some more later on, but we are having hard time. I been in Port Arthur twelve year now and have lost some children by typhoid and fever. There is my boy there (pointing to his son). He is eighteen year old and was verra sick not long ago, and nearly died. Dat is not good, big boy like him, and it cost much money to get him well again.

Although living conditions in the Old Country were as primitive as those in the coal docks, life at home had been lived outdoors; each day the men had descended the slopes to work in the fields below. The *bordanti* were not accustomed to the indoor life of a long cold winter. Nevertheless, they accepted the congestion of the boarding house in order to enjoy the familiar food, language and the congenial warmth of each other's company. It was also far preferable to the saloons. They passed their time playing cards and making music on their accordions, guitars, mandolins, and violins. They sang and joked. And they smoked incessantly. If the boarding house included *bordanti* from different parts of Italy, there was a lively banter, perhaps verbal clashes and even fistfights. North-South hatreds as well as regional rivalries were long bred in Italy. Thus, the *bordanti* clustered together according to their province, not so much as Italian nationals, but as people of hometowns — as *paesani* (kinsmen). The Southern Italians tended to locate in Port Arthur and the Northerners in Fort William.

Luigi and his cousin, John Covello, loved to sing and undoubtedly whiled away many winter hours doing so. They sang the popular Italian love songs: "O Sole Mio," "Santa Lucia," and "Torna a Surriento." During the war years they sang English war songs such as "Over There," "Pack Up Your Troubles in Your Old Kit Bag," "Keep the Home Fires Burning," and "Mademoiselle from Armentières." I have a hard-covered, dark green ledger that belonged to Luigi in which the words to the song "It's a Long Way to Tipperary" were handwritten and signed by "Hilda Anderson," perhaps a friend.

But dancing was Luigi's great obsession. According to a 1913 survey by the local Methodist Church, "the dance halls were supervised by responsible persons" and were "without bad influences." Luigi frequented dance halls, such as the Orpheum Hall on Cooke Street and Barton & Fisher Hall on Algoma Street, where qualified instructors taught new dances to the music of the Shuttleworth, Whitehouse or Manning Orchestras. Luigi knew the three-step and four-step, the mazurka, the waltz, the fox trot, the schottische and polka. He was smooth. He was graceful. Not surprisingly, he was invited to dance at the exclusive Shuniah Club on the top floor of the Whalen Building. In his fancy dress shirts and silk bow ties, Luigi must have cut a fine figure dancing to such tunes as "If You Were the Only Girl in the World," "I'm Always Chasing Rainbows," and "Alice Blue Gown." He always showed his partner respect by placing a handkerchief between his hand and her back. Such a gentleman.

Card playing was another of his favourite pastimes, and he was equally adept at the Italian games of *scopa* and *briscola*, or North American cribbage or poker. The men played seven days a week, not realizing that playing cards on the Sabbath day was forbidden. On September 19, 1919 the following item appeared in the local paper:

> Seven foreigners charged with playing cards on the Lord's Day were fined $15 and costs each by Magistrate Palling in the Fort William court this morning.

The young Italians had to contend not only with the harsh climate and rugged environment but also with the strange customs of the English.

At this point, the Roman Catholic Church did not play a significant role in the lives of the *bordanti*. Although marriages were solemnized in church, attendance at Sunday mass and at other services was poor. The *bordanti* would more likely be playing cards than attending Sunday mass. Calabrese men were traditionally anti-clerical, and religion was considered a woman's affair.

Initially, the majority of young Italians had no intention of remaining permanently in America, which from their point of view was one vast amorphous place — Buenos Aires or Montivideo, New York or Canada. They worked their seasonal jobs, coming and going whenever and wherever they pleased, pilgrims in strange lands. Their sole aim was to earn *pezze* (dollars), in order to return home where they could live like *signori* (gentlemen). Back home, the *pezza* soon evolved into an important symbol of America, and actually had concrete purchasing power in the isolated mountain villages of Calabria.

Ironically, Canadian government policy, under the influence of British racialist theories, discouraged the permanent settlement of Italians. Sir Clifford Sifton, the Minister of the Interior from 1896 to 1905 — and the man instrumental in launching the vigorous campaign in Great Britain and continental Europe to settle Canada's West — had grave doubts about the quality and the cultural acceptability of the Southern Europeans. He went so far as to say: "No steps are to be taken to assist or encourage Italian immigration to Canada." Other ethnic groups had the advantage of organized colonization schemes and the promise of free or inexpensive land. (American intolerance was even worse. A New York paper went so far as to refer to Italian immigrants as "steerage slime.")

The Italian government showed little or no concern over this. In Canada, the Italian consulates were staffed largely by Northen Italian bureaucrats who viewed the immigrants with condescension, since many of them originated from *bassa Italia* (Southern Italy) with its pervasive poverty, overpopulation and illiteracy. Nor did the church offer any social services or opportunities to learn English.

During the first years of the mass movement of Italian labourers to Canada, an Italian employment agent known as a *padrone* acted as a go-between for the prospective employer and the immigrant. The *padrone* was essential to the workers who could not speak English and were, in most cases, illiterate in their own language. The bilingual *padrone* functioned as the labourer's letter-writer, banker, interpreter, and personal advisor. Although the *padrone* system worked, it was, unfortunately, riddled by agents who were not averse to exploiting their countrymen for personal gain and power.

The Italians may have been "illiterate and superstitious;" they may have lacked the social graces and had garlic breath, unshaven faces and shabby clothes; they may even have been noisy and boisterous; but they provided the cheap manual labour necessary to harnessing the bountiful wilderness for industry and commerce. The English got all the best jobs, while the Italians were left the pick-and-shovel work. With their strong backs and shoulders, they performed the dangerous, dirty and heavy labours scorned by *gli Inglesi*.

The Italian immigrants knew the secret of success lay in two words: hard work. The young were trained from early childhood to long working hours. They matured early and even as teenagers regarded themselves as men. To work was to show proof of manhood. So strong was the belief in work that it governed behaviour quite apart from considerations of monetary gain. To be able to work — to have a *giobba* — was a matter of pride. I was told about one migrant who stayed up all night on the roof of the CNR freight shed playing his twelve-string guitar in order to be the first hired the next morning.

With the strength of their bodies, the Italians built the railways, docks, roads, bridges, breakwaters and sewers of Northern Ontario. With picks and shovels and axes they confronted the world's oldest rock. They drilled deep, loaded dynamite into the holes, and blasted away. Their rock-cuts scarred forever the face of the ancient rock. Man's strength pitted against the strength of nature. The physical exertion alone made them feel alive and proud, and it is doubtful that their pitiless battering of the storied northern forest ever occurred to them as anything but productive labour.

The British Empire was forging a nation, and the young Dominion paid no heed to its indigenous people — they who lived in intimate harmony with the natural rhythms of the earth.

But the wilderness had its own inscrutable will, and man's destruction required constant maintenance. The Italians had to keep grading and ballasting the rail beds. Although these jobs were considered unskilled, a background of experience was essential if the work was to be done intelligently. Conditioned from boyhood to handle the *zappa* — a simple farm tool which they used to shore up the earth on their rocky fields back home, and to repair the stone fencing on their mountain slopes — they were singularly qualified for excavation and rock work. They soon established a solid reputation for these skills. Along with their remarkable endurance, sobriety and cheerfulness, these qualities made them attractive to hard-boiled employers who paid no attention to negative stereotypes as long as the men worked well in their tight homogeneous groups.

Their original purpose in coming to America may have been to earn enough money to enable their families to live better in Calabria. But the young immigrants soon began to prefer the freedom and opportunities of the New World. They liked the white bread and coffee. Only the rich in Calabria could afford these. Among the peasants, coffee was given only to the sick — and a thimbleful at that. They liked the conveniences of North American life — private toilets, electric lights, and running water, one of the great wonders of America. They could find spring water almost anywhere and running water with just the twist of a tap.

During the early century, living conditions among the peasantry of Calabria were miserable. Life was an endless struggle perpetually strained by a poor water and sewage supply, a lack of power and communication systems, bad roads, impassable mountains, poor soil exhausted by centuries of abuse and the ravages of earthquakes, landslides and volcanic eruptions, as well as excessive and abusive taxes.

Despite victimization by religious, ethnic and class prejudice, a hostile climate — not to mention strong ties with their hometowns — many Italians decided to stay permanently in the North. The men sent for their families or married the Italian girls who trickled into the city.

They were not interested in being farmers. They may have come from an agriculture background; they may have missed their grapevines, fruit and nut trees — olives, figs, almonds, chestnuts; but farming in Calabria, with its stubborn and dry clay soil, its sudden hills and steep-walled valleys, was a struggle from which the young migrants wanted to escape. They preferred road and rail work to farming. And they liked the ready cash.

Besides, Canada was a place of businessmen. The goal of the more ambitious was to own a small business. The Sisco brothers had arrived as young boys without any knowledge of the language, customs, laws or politics of Canada. They had worked for a few years as labourers. But, like a number of the more enterprising Italians, they soon advanced.

It wasn't easy. Their lives were simple and their wants few. And they made few demands. With the strictest economy, they were able to save enough money to start their own grocery and confectionery stores. They were particularly adept at merchandising fruits and vegetables. Giovanni Sisco earned distinction as one of the first to bring ice-cream (via Duluth) to the Twin Cities.

By the 1920s many Italians had opened up small fruit and confectionery stores, shoe repair shops and barber shops. Some started tobacco and cigar shops, ice cream parlours, shoe shine shops and pool rooms. Despite having to work long hours, often with family assistance, ownership gave them a feeling of independence they had not known in Italy.

Despite their entrance into the business world, the immigrants were still considered part of Port Arthur's "unskilled labour force" and held in low esteem. Port Arthur was governed by a ruling class of British stock. Many were descended from the early settlers and had grown up with the city. They controlled local political and economic life until after World War II.

Class barriers were strong. A well-defined pecking order of prejudice separated the English who were on top from the Italians who were at the bottom. (The Finns and Scandinavians constituted "the aristocracy" of the immigrant population). With their dark skins, heavy accents, work-roughened hands and dirty work clothes, the Italians were the visible minority of the day.

An article in the August 10, 1918 issue of the *Daily News-Chronicle* criticized Italian males for resenting the poll tax when they were often seen "peeling off" large bills. The fondness of Italian males for large bills was no more than a mask of bravado. For all their swagger, they were confused by, and ignorant of, Port Arthur's cultural norms.

The English upper classes kept themselves aloof and enjoyed their social activities secluded from "the foreigners." The society pages of the local paper recorded their many social events and often listed the names of those in attendance. No Italian names appeared. None sailed on the moonlight excursions on the S.S. Saronic, sponsored by the Junior Daughters of the Empire. None attended the many garden parties, verandah teas, musical teas and tea dances on Saturday afternoons.

None belonged to the Art and Literature Club which heard addresses on topics such as "Belgian Cathedrals," "The Worth and Work of Women," and "The Art of Living." None heard lectures given by distinguished persons such as Nellie McClung and Vilhjalmur Stefansson, the famous Arctic explorer. Stefansson compared the Eskimo to the good-natured childlike Southern Italians, as had *The New York Times*, in 1862, reporting the appearance of an Eskimo who looked "for all the world like a South Italian in North Pole uniform."

No Italian sang with the Port Arthur Women's Musical Club, which studied Japanese music and listened to vocals, such as "My Lady's Bower," "Moon of My Delight" and "Cupid at the Ferry." None were in the Women's Press Club, Women's Canadian Club, the Port Arthur Philharmonic Club, which staged the annual Messiah, or the St. Patrick's Dramatic Club, which in 1918 presented *Kathleen Mavourneen*, "a refined Irish comedy." None were in local amateur productions such as *Isolanthe* and *The Mikado*.

But there was hope. On March 31, 1917, Ralph Colosimo played a clarinet solo *La Sonnambula* by Bellini with the Port Arthur City Band and on March 15, 1920, at the Lyceum Theatre, Luigi Sprovieri played a euphonium solo, "Beneath Thy Window."

Luckily, few in the North would have seen the following advertisement of the Essex Canning and Preserving Company in Toronto:

> We do not employ Italian labour but confine all our employees to resident families of Essex, with their old-fashioned ideas of cleanliness in the preparation of any food produce.

An article in the *Daily News-Chronicle* of March 10, 1920 recorded the xenophobic attitudes that a number of Port Arthur's leading citizens harboured against the "newcomers." The Mayor claimed that "if Canadians fail to do their duty in making citizens of the foreigners, Canadians will be assimilated by them."

The President of the Port Arthur-Fort William Rotary Club said: "All boys and girls born in the coal docks miss something that we have had as boys and girls — an inherited idea of law, order and constitutional government!"

The President of the Kiwanis declared that the foreign population in Canada, as he knew it at present, was a menace. "The majority of enemies to organized government in the country are foreign-born or born of foreign parents."

By 1920, race assimilation was a problem of national importance. So many non-English immigrants were now permanently settled in Canada that the "foreign" population of Vancouver was 65%, Regina 78% and the Twin Cities 59%. The previous year, the Imperial Order of the Daughters of the Empire had passed resolutions advocating a Canadianization campaign to:

> ... propagate British ideals and institutions, to ... banish old world points of view ... and to make new Canadians ... one hundred percent British in language, thought, feeling and impulse.

A policy of Anglo-conformity was actively promoted. It permitted little cultural deviation. On October 17, 1921 a news report in the local paper informed its readers that

> In Port Arthur police court this morning 3 Italian women were charged with trespassing on the CNR property. These women were found sweeping out the grain from the empty grain cars when found by the police. They were each fined $4 and costs.

A woman in court was unheard of in Calabria. To be fined for salvaging grain that would otherwise be wasted was unimaginable. What was honourable in Calabria was criminal in Canada. All they could do was mutter in exasperation: *Mannaggia l'America!* (an expression that connotes the high price America exacts from its immigrants.) The cold stares of the court revealed contempt for everything the women stood for, including their black shawls, black stockings and black dresses. No wonder they referred to the English as *gente dura, gente fredda* (callous people, cold people).

In 1921, as part of a vigorous campaign urging people to own their own homes, the Port Arthur Real Estate Board ran the following advertisement — a little more subtle than some messages imparted by the privileged sector:

> "My Papa owns his home," a little blue-eyed girl proudly proclaims to her schoolmates. And immediately one or two others shout, "So does mine." "Mine does too." The rest hang their heads and say nothing. Which will your child do?

The Italians, no strangers to a class-stratified society, were by no means cowed by the discrimination. On March 21, 1920, his birthday, Luigi bought his own home at 147 Secord Street for $2,000. The street was named after the Southern Ontario heroine, Laura Secord, who saved British Canada from the Americans in the War of 1812. His neighbours had "English" names — Janet Williams, William Baker, John Walker, Frank McDonald, Elford Wray, William Gordon, John W. McIntyre and John T. Barden. Within eight years after returning to Canada, Luigi had managed to save enough money to buy his home and send for his younger sister Virginia. He showered her with gifts and set her up as his chatelaine.

The Italians were also asserting their ethnic individuality, as witnessed in this exhortation from the local paper for October 20, 1921.

> Annual Dinner in aid of St. Anthony's Church. The Armouries. Dance after 8 o'clock. Macaroni and spaghetti *à la Italienne*. Learn how really delicious two Italian national dishes are. Guttridge Orchestra.

Whether the French spelling was used to upgrade the Italian dish, I am not sure.

In 1920, soon after her arrival in Port Arthur, Luisa Sisco met Luigi Petrone in her brother Giovanni's store. She had clear blue eyes and wavy hair, the colour of chestnuts. Although she had known the Petrone family in Calabria she had never met Luigi. Over a period of months Luigi watched her and eventually plucked enough courage to ask Giovanni for Luisa's hand in marriage. Giovanni, in turn, asked if she wanted Luigi. Luisa knew that if she objected, her brother would not force her into a marriage. But why should she object? "What kind of man is he?" she asked. "*Un grande lavoratore*" (A good worker) was the reply. That was good enough for Luisa. There was no courting. Proper female behaviour did not allow the two to be seen walking together before the sacred bonds of matrimony had been solemnized.

Luigi Petrone and Luisa Sisco were married at St. Anthony's Church on January 5, 1922. She was twenty-five, he thirty-two. Their wedding picture shows a serious couple elegantly dressed. The bride wore a calf-length white satin dress which she had designed and made herself, a white lace veil arranged with a chaplet of orange blossoms, white stockings, shoes and gloves. She carried a shower bouquet of white roses and fern tied with long white satin ribbons. The groom wore a dark suit, a stiff formal collar, white silk bow tie, white gloves and white boutonniere.

Luisa's maid of honour, Luigi's sister, Virginia, dressed exactly like the bride but wore a wide-brimmed white silk hat made by Fanny Albanese, a neighbour. Both bride and maid of honour wore blue sapphire pendants on thin gold chains, gifts from the groom. The bride's two nieces, Giovanni's daughter, Madeline, and Giustino's daughter, Doris, were flower girls, in short white dresses and veils, white stockings, white high-laced boots and white mittens. Each carried a cone-shaped bouquet of red roses.

The wedding reception was held in Luigi's home. Maria Rigato who was eleven at the time remembers:

> It was a very cold day — you can see I'm wearing spats in the wedding picture, but it was warm and fun in the house. My mother

Teresina, who was from your father's home town, was in charge of the food preparation. There must have been at least sixty people. I can remember mother frying meatballs and stewing pork and chicken and making spaghetti. Somebody played the accordion and people danced all night. Your mother was very reserved.

And so it was that Luisa Sisco arrived at 147 Secord Street.

3
Mamma

I do not know anything about my infancy. I do not know the hour of my birth, nor my weight and length. We did not ask such questions as kids do nowadays. Mamma told me, however, that during the first year of my life, as dictated by tradition, she wrapped me up tightly from head to toe with layer upon layer of cloth strips, *fasce*, binding me in order that I would grow straight and not move my arms and legs.

Mamma gave birth to five more children: Alfred Antonio a year later, Frank Leonard a year and a half after that and Rita Antonia, a year and a half after Frank. My youngest sister, Mary, was born after a baby boy had died at birth in St. Joseph's Hospital, strangled by his own umbilical cord.

Nurses have told me that Italian women in labour do not bear pain quietly but scream with abandon. Perhaps that is why the nurses in attendance may not have been too concerned when Mamma kept screaming during the birth of what would have been her fifth child. They arrived at her bedside too late.

Mamma was a woman of great intelligence and inner strength, resourceful and adaptable, but above all else pragmatic. She was a Juno, the stately and powerful Roman matron who presided over the household and the well-being of her family. She was the stabilizing and unifying focus of the family, the bond that made all life possible.

Before it became environmentally trendy, Mamma was a master of conservation. She was also a master of *arrangiarsi*, the art of making ends meet, "making do" and adjusting to any circumstance. At the time, there was no unemployment insurance, no family allowances, and Daddy did not have a steady job that guaranteed a regular income. She could stretch one dollar into twenty.

She recycled, remodelled, repaired, and reused everything in sight. She washed flour, sugar and cement bags in a lye solution and hung them out on the clothesline to bleach in the sun. She made flour-bag sheets and pillowcases and sugar-bag tablecloths and napkins. She made cement-bag tea towels and camisoles for herself. She made cement bag pillows and filled them with chicken feathers. On a few I can still see the faded lettering which had refused to bleach out. She made dresses from flour bags for her three girls. She crocheted a lace collar here, a border there, and tied on a ribbon. Or she sewed on coloured buttons and puff sleeves, sometimes reusing old thread. She patched and repatched Daddy's Stanfield underwear and her own bloomers at the crotch. The workmanship was so fine that the stitches would have been difficult to find.

After we were older she would buy a bolt of cotton and make identical dresses for Rita, Mary and me. She always checked to see whether she had been sold the correct yardage. She used her own system of measurement: the distance from the top of her nose to the end of her outstretched arm was roughly a yard. And she cut her own patterns from newspapers.

One winter when I was twelve or thirteen, Mamma must have bought Eaton's entire supply of red, green and white balls of wool. She made the girls tricolour toques, mitts, scarves and dickies. I refused to wear mine. "These are the colours of the Italian flag," she protested. "I am not Italian. I am *Canadese*. I am a Canadian. I am a Canadian," I tried to explain. It was no use. Once I was out of Mamma's sight, I would remove the garments and hide them under the porch steps. I preferred the winter's cold to the ridicule of my schoolmates. On another occasion she knitted me a lime green suit of the finest wool with an orange angora Peter Pan collar. The girls at school were not wearing hand-knitted suits, and after one wearing, I refused to wear mine. Alfred recalls his embarrassment each time his high school class stood up to sing *God Save the King* because of the patches on the seat of his pants, which he tried to hide with the palms of his hands. Mamma could not understand why we were ashamed of our patches, or our hand made clothes, because, in the Italian mind, they were marks of a woman's management skills.

Mamma's knitting and crocheting always won her prizes at the Canadian Lakehead Exhibition. I recall a rust-coloured suit Mamma knitted for Mary, for which she won second prize. When she wore the suit, I thought she looked like Shirley Temple. Mary had golden hair which Mamma used to put up in rags to make ringlets. I was so proud of her because she did not look Italian.

When I was older, Mamma's finely shaped, capable hands intrigued me. Never still, they moved with quiet skill and speed — darning, sewing, crocheting, knitting, patching, mending, and embroidering. She could knit a pair of mittens overnight. Whether at her whirring Singer treadle sewing machine or sewing by hand, she worked with a flair. I can still see her threading her needle. She would wet the thumb and index finger of her right hand with her tongue in order to twist the thread so that it would go through the eye of the needle. Mamma could not sew without the silver thimble she had brought with her from Italy. She used it throughout her life and I have it now. For her, using a thimble was the mark of a good seamstress. I sewed without one, using long strands of thread to finish more quickly, so I thought. Even her Calabrese maxim, "*Chine infile l'ago con il filo lungo è vagabonda*" (whoever threads the needle with a long thread is lazy) did not deter me. I inherited her jars of buttons and old zippers but not her gifted hands. I never did learn to hold my knitting needles properly or keep my crochet needle at the correct angle. My three youthful productions included a crocheted collar, a knitted dickey and an embroidered tablecloth. But these were botched with frightful errors that were too much for Mamma's patience, and we both gave up.

Mamma's economies extended to every phase of our lives. She kept glass sealers for re-use year after year. She had Daddy cut off the tops of salad oil cans for planting tomatoes and herbs. She sent nothing to the laundry or dry-cleaners. I can recall that stretching our lace curtains on a wooden frame was a whole day's work for her. She even half-soled our shoes with tough cardboard patches.

One Christmas, when each of us kids received a hamper of toys from Alfred's *compare* (godfather), Mamma returned the gifts which had been bought at Marshall-Wells, exchanging them for an assortment of kitchen utensils. And when we received boxes of chocolates, she stored them in her trunk, where her linens were protected by moth-balls, to use them as gifts, or to serve to guests. I recall my mortification when a friend told me that our chocolates always smelled of mothballs. It was a Calabrese custom to put aside a portion of goods for the circulation of gifts and reciprocal giving. "You can't have one arm longer than the other" ("*Na mano curta e natra lunga*") was her stock advice — a short arm when you're giving but a long arm when you are receiving. "And remember," she would add, "*Chine mangia sulu s'affuca*" (Whoever eats alone chokes.)

Our education was expensive. Although public school students received all their school supplies free, Catholic school students did not. Consequently, Mamma had to pay for the textbooks, scribblers, pens, pencils, erasers, rulers, art paper, boxes of paints, all the school needs for her five children, who, eventually, were all going to school at the same time. One pencil, one eraser, and one ruler had to last each of us the whole year. I had to make the margins of my scribbler narrow to have more space to write. In addition, Mamma paid for Alfred's violin, my piano, and Rita's singing and dancing lessons. Regardless of the cost, she was making sure that her children were getting a well-rounded education.

Mamma also was saving to buy a brick house that would match the *palazzo* of her childhood. And money had to be put in the bank as a safeguard for emergencies and to get us through the winter months when Daddy was out of work. It was the custom to "run a bill" for groceries, but apart from the grocery bill, Mamma bought nothing on credit. She stressed the importance of "money in the bank," instilling in each of us financial responsibility and independence. "*La vutta si speragna quon'è china*" (The flagon of wine is saved when it's full), was her constant exhortation. Family prudence was so instilled in us that we each had our own bank accounts. And by the time I was sixteen Mamma owned an apartment building.

She was the family doctor, too, a believer in simple home remedies. There was no socialized medicine then, and each doctor's call cost money. Her staples were iodine, castor oil and epsom salts. She kept chicken fat in a jar for bruises, and used honey for sore throats. Heat was a cure-all: a hot-water bottle, warmed-up olive oil to rub hard on sprains, or the heat of mustard plasters and Rawleigh's red ointment. For years Mamma covered Daddy's aching back with red flannel while pressing it with a hot iron. And she believed, too, that her nightly tot of brandy was good medicine for Daddy and herself.

Apart from holy medals, Mamma did not rely on healing charms as some Calabrese mothers did. She did take advantage of a neighbourhood woman reputed to have miraculous hands. I recall Mamma summoning her to *apparare* (massage) Daddy's back.

Mamma's relatives from Piane Crati often sent her flowers of the camomile plant which were supposed to help calm the nerves, relieve coughs and stomach aches. Whenever she tried to give them to me, however, I refused, deeming anything Italian inferior.

Mamma's garden filled our backyard. Having inherited the Calabrese's ingenious use of available space, she wasted no soil on plants which could not be eaten. She made every foothold of soil bear fruit. She took pleasure in flowers only when she arranged them for the church altar. Our Finnish neighbour had sweet peas, bleeding hearts, cosmos and nasturtiums in her front and backyards while I had to be content with the two lilac bushes that grew on the corners of our frontyard. I gazed longingly on her strawberry and raspberry bushes which spread along our backyard fence and picked the berries, making sure she never caught me.

Mamma did not keep plants in the house. A friend once gave us three magnificently curly silk mums. I put them in a glass vase on the dining room table and for years dusted them lovingly.

Traditionally, Italian families are lavish in celebrating rituals of passage such as baptism, holy communion and confirmation. With five children Mamma thought such celebrations extravagant. At eight years of age I received my first holy communion dressed in Mamma's wedding veil and dress which she had hemmed up. Two years later when I made my confirmation, Mamma let down the wedding dress. It wasn't the dress I was ashamed of, it was my shoes — my dark scruffy every-day shoes. All I could see were the new white and black patent leather shoes of the other girls.

Mamma did allow herself a few luxuries. In the isolated rural areas of Southern Italy where the same customs continued down the centuries, women of the *contadina* class did not wear hats. They wore only black scarves. But while I was growing up I never once saw Mamma's head covered with a scarf. In fact, she loved matching hats and gloves. She never went out in public without them. And she always spent money on the best of inner garments. Her figure was firm, and her carriage was regal from years of balancing jugs of water on her head during her youth. Mamma enjoyed being well-dressed.

Only once in my life did I ask Mamma for money. It was for a contest that came advertised in the mail from New York. I had to unscramble the names of over thirty movie stars. An automobile was the grand prize. I knew I could do it. After several nights of hard work, I had unscrambled all the names in the booklet. I leapt for joy. The car was mine.

A letter eventually came confirming it. I didn't read past the first sentence. I went immediately to Mamma and announced my good fortune. I presented her with the proof. When I read on, however, I discovered to my shock, that a payment of one dollar was required to facilitate the prize-giving. I hesitated to ask Mamma for it. But as soon as I did, to my surprise, she gave it to me.

Soon, another letter requesting an additional dollar arrived. I did not ask Mamma for it. Eventually the letters stopped coming. I was about fifteen at the time and I was ashamed of myself for having wasted Mamma's dollar. She never brought it up, and to this day I am mystified as to why. I have never entered another contest.

Children in Southern Italian families were expected to contribute to the family income. "A father with many children is like a king with many vassals" was the Calabrese saying. From the age of seven both Alfred and Franki helped supplement Daddy's earnings. They sold newspapers and magazines, set bowling pins, and brought home scavenged herring. There were no soft residential paper routes for the Italian boys. Those went to *l'Inglese*. But it didn't bother my brothers. As soon as Alfred was let out of school, he would run non-stop to the *News-Chronicle* building on Lorne Street to buy his papers for three cents each. (They were sold for a nickel.) The competition for vending sites was fierce. The older Italian boys, the Uvanelis, Feros, Agostinos, and Veltris claimed territorial jurisdiction over the most profitable sidewalk corners like the Prince Arthur Hotel corner at Cumberland and Arthur. Alfred did not dare invade their turf because street justice prevailed. As a result, he had to hustle, plan his strategies and outwit his competition. It was crucial to be first on the street and in and out of restaurants quickly. In the summertime he would sneak on board the passenger liners. He had to work fast — sell his first batch of papers, go to the *News-Chronicle* for a second batch, and if sales were brisk go for a third batch. He boarded grain ships and freighters. On the way home, he stopped at the big hotels:

The Marriaggi, Kimberley, Princess, Donati, Laprade, Vendome, and CN. He stopped at the cafés, as the restaurants were called: the Port Arthur, Stanley, Diamond, Twin City, Devon, Murray and Popular. I called him the gingerbread boy because he was always running. Being under age, Alfred had to humour the bartenders who were supposed to chase him out of the beer parlours. He also had to charm the policemen on the beat: Strawson, Radford, O'Connor and Hutchinson. A Cumberland Street prostitute kept calling him to save his nickels and dimes and to "come up and see me some time." (Alfred told me this just recently.)

Mamma expected the boys home by 6:30 for supper. I can remember the three girls seated at the table waiting for their arrival so that we could begin to eat. If the boys were not home by 7:00, Mamma would put on her hat and coat and go looking for them.

Alfred and Franki also sold popular magazines like *Liberty*, the *Saturday Evening Post* and the *Ladies Home Journal*. Twice the boys won top prizes for highest sales. From the prizes offered on the first occasion, they selected the family's first toaster. Next came a pale blue dresser set with a floral design for me. I can still see it.

When they were older they would go out after supper to Gibson's Bowling Alley to set pins until 11 p.m. All their earnings went to Mamma.

The late Fall was the time when commercial fishermen brought in their herring catch. Alfred and Franki would grab any fish that fell from the boxes as they were being transported on to the dock or any that they could "liberate." They would sell some to the neighbourhood Finns for five cents each.

Although Mamma did not push her girls to find work outside the home, she never gave us any spending money either. We had to earn our few nickels after school somehow, and when I was about nine I got a secret job. I made five cents a page pronouncing the words which Charlie the Chinaman had written in columns on pages of a scribbler. Charlie owned a hand laundry next door to Joe Holomego, the shoemaker on Bay Street, across from the Finn Hall. It took all my courage to enter the laundry and walk through a huge room that was always in semi-darkness and filled with steam from washing troughs, water buckets and irons. I was frightened of customers coming in and catching me there and telling Mamma. I tried to appear cool and calm, camouflaging my fear from Charlie, praying that he would take less time with each word as he repeated it after me.

Somehow Alfred and Franki found out where I was getting my nickels, and each time I had something on them, they would threaten to tell Mamma by chanting:

Chinky Chinky Chinaman
Wash my pants
Put them in the boiler
And make them dance.

They kept up this blackmail even after I had stopped my education of Charlie.

I did not know it then, but Alfred told me recently that the large dingy laundry room was also an opium den. As a street-smart adolescent, he enjoyed peeking in the cracks of the doorway on Sunday afternoons to watch with fascination as Charlie and his friends smoked long-stemmed wooden pipes hooked to a water bucket.

I found other sources of money, too. I combed the alleys for empty bottles and sold them for a copper each at Barton & Fisher Hardware. When they did not want any more, I discovered another hardware store in the next block on Bay Street. I tried to keep my new found source of money secret, but Rita followed me one day, and I lost my monopoly.

With Mamma's permission we also sold lettuce, radishes and onions from her garden at five cents a bunch. Mary and Rita had regular customers in the neighbourhood, while I had to venture up the Bay Street steps into the Mariday Park area where the rich people lived. High, Summit and Winnipeg Avenues were a strange world of large houses and streets empty of pedestrians. The stillness frightened me. I was self-conscious when I rapped on the doors.

Business was never good, and Mama wondered whether the English ever ate garden fresh salads. After two or three forays, I stopped.

When I was desperate, I plucked enough courage to approach the lumberjacks who stood around the Finn Hall and beg for nickels in Finn: *Anna minulle nikkeli*. I never told Mamma and she never found out. When I got older I scrubbed the cold linoleum floors and bare boards of a rooming house in the neighbourhood for fifty cents.

The conspicuous consumerism of today didn't exist, and my wants were few. My brothers brought home the Sunday funnies and movie magazines. But I always craved candy. Every summer day I stood, my nose pressed against the window of Peanut Jim's, carefully picking out the candy I would buy if I had a nickel. There were butterscotch kisses, maple buds, licorice pipes and cigars, lemon jellies, black balls and big red wax lips with white teeth to chew and chew. To have a nickel to buy enough one-cent candies to fill a small brown paper bag was sheer heaven.

One summer I found an American dollar bill on the board sidewalk of Memorial Avenue. I wanted to tell everybody but didn't, making my dollar last a whole year, buying caramel suckers, two for a nickel. Each day I rationed myself to a few licks. I can still remember walking down Secord Street and up Wiley Street Hill to my music lesson, licking my caramel sucker. My music teacher's mother kept it for me on a piece of wax paper on the newel post in the front hall, where I picked it up again after my lesson to lick on the way home.

As I look back now, it seems that we lived below our financial means. Daddy's work was irregular but he must have made good money when he did work. Mamma who was intensely frugal probably put a large portion of it in the bank. In the Southern Italian mind-set, a person who displays his money risks attracting the jealous fates. Mamma deliberately avoided ostentation for fear of the community's ill will. Peasant society in Calabria was strongly egalitarian. To consider oneself superior was to show *superbia* and would be ridiculed. Secrecy over one's success guarded against any loss. As Mamma was accustomed to reminding me *"Chi ti sa ti apra"* (Whoever knows you, opens you).

As a single man and during the early years of his marriage, Daddy had often lent money to his friends. This invariably ended in both the loss of the money and the friend — and Mamma's displeasure over the money. Daddy's spirit was large and generous, and Mamma accused him of lacking natural cunning; he was not *furbo* (foxy) enough.

Mamma's perspective was the legacy of a long history of military and political suppression in Southern Italy. For centuries, the people had to cope with local princelings, petty despots, papal legates, Spanish viceroys, the Bourbons and Italian bureaucrats. To deal with the outside world they were forced to be shrewd. Astuteness or *furberia* was a method of survival. As far as Mamma was concerned, to be too good was to be a *fesso* (fool), and could ruin oneself and one's family. Life was hard, without mercy.

When I was ten years old, an Italian shoe maker with whom Daddy had a business arrangement repaid a debt to Daddy with shoes. A hundred shoe boxes were stacked into a big closet in our dining room. As soon as my chums found out that I had this bonanza at my disposal, they wanted to play with me. We would open box after box to find the high heels that we liked. How Mamma hated those shoes! Not once did she try to find a pair that fit her.

For years, Mamma and Daddy argued about Daddy's disastrous financial ventures. Mamma saw herself as the *Madonna Addolorata* (Mother Sorrowful) bearing each new setback with stoic endurance.

When I was about sixteen she made a momentous decision. Although she had, for years, controlled the family's budget, her husband's paycheque, and the earnings of her boys, she had displayed, as required by custom and church law, deference and obedience to her husband. But the time had come for her to take charge. She was going to invest the family's modest savings. Although she believed that the Lord would provide for those who loved Him, she was pragmatic enough to realize that

God helps those who help themselves. She may have often quoted the Calabrese adage, *Dammi fortuna e iettami a mare* (Give me fortune and throw me into the sea), but she also knew that fortune favors the bold.

But how best to begin investing? One day in 1939, the answer became clear when Mamma noticed a sign on the window of the Canadian Bank of Commerce: *Money To Lend*. Southern Italians tended to distrust bankers, and until then Mamma had not known that banks *lent* money. She entered the bank and asked for the manager. A few days later, convinced of her financial accountability, he loaned her the money to buy the Anderson Block on the South-west corner of Algoma and Cornwall. Mamma had become a landlady. This was a courageous venture for Mamma who came from a people so cautious that the common response to a query about one's health was *menza sita e menza caposceola* (between fine and rough silk).

How efficient she was! She kept the accounts, collected the rents, wrote out the receipts, paid the bills, figured out the mortgage interest. She placed great importance on signing her name, and I can still see that final deliberate flourish with her pen. With her family's help, Mamma maintained "the block." During the winter it required daily care; snow had to be shovelled, ice chipped away, the coal furnace filled, fired, stoked, and the ashes hauled out.

Because Daddy worked out of town while I was growing up, the burden of disciplining five rambunctious children fell on Mamma. Italian parents could be very strict but Mamma's authority was never severe. She tried to govern us by proverbs: *Chi sputa in cielo in faccia ritorna* (Don't spit in the wind, because it can hit you in the face); *Dicemi con chine stai ca ti dico chine si* (Tell me who you go with and I'll tell you who you are); *A lingua no na osse ma osse taglia* (The tongue has no bones but it can cut bones). And she used folk tales. I remember the story about the ant and the cicada — the cicada who did not work during the summer but sang her heart out, and the ant who worked and worked and worked. When winter came the cicada had to go to the ant for food. But the ant told her to go eat her songs. When neither proverb nor folk-tale worked, Mamma threatened us into good behaviour. She warned us that she would report us to the policeman on the neighbourhood beat who would record our names in his little black notebook. If our names were recorded five times we would be sent to jail.

Vehemence of speech is common among Southern Italians. Mamma would scream such Calabrese expletives as *saraceno*, a term of abuse dating back to the time when the Saracen hordes conquered Calabria, and other insults such as *faci tosta*, *scustamata*, and *dizgraziata*.

In my child arrogance, I was embarrassed more by her high-pitched "foreign" voice than by what she was saying.

In a Calabrese family, scolding was often accompanied by the most violent threats. But Mamma did not hurl curses such as *chi vo fare la morte du cane* (May you die the death of a dog). Cruelty to animals, especially dogs and cats who were not productive, was common in Mamma's time. Dogs would literally starve to death.

Open quarrelling with family elders and going out on dates were regarded as the ways of a *puttana* (whore), a label of contempt commonly used by Italian parents to make their rebellious daughters feel dirty and cheap. Mamma never called me *puttana*.

More than any other people, the Calabrese speak without words. During hundreds of years of foreign domination, they developed elaborate codes of body language, and I can recall Mamma using two dramatic gestures to show her anger. She would bite the knuckle of her index finger to show rage and flick the fingertips of one hand under the chin to show contempt.

When we had taxed her patience beyond the limit, entirely overwhelming her, Mamma would become hysterical and throw herself to the floor. My brothers and sisters would vanish. Guilt-ridden and frightened that Mamma was going to die, I would try to revive her, promising we would never, never be "bad" again. I can't recall how many times she did this, but I remember that she would stay on the floor until she was obliged to get up when visitors or salesmen arrived, for instance, the Fuller Brush or Rawleigh man.

In fact, when I was growing up I lived in constant fear of Mamma dying. She was always ailing in one way or another, and indeed during her 40's she was operated on for gall stones and varicose veins. Whatever the true severity of her sicknesses, she, like other Southern Italian women, had the habit of saying *staiu morennu* (I'm dying).

Southern Italians tend to exaggerate their emotions. I can still recall Mamma wailing "*Sciullu mio*" (Woe is me) and tearing at her hair so hard when her brother Ciccilo died that she lost one of her treasured gold earrings. Even a trivial matter could bring on the histrionics. Later, when I was a young woman, I would rebuke Mamma for this emotional excess. But her reply was invariably a request to allow her to *spurgare* (give vent to her feelings). Ingrained in her was the Calabrese attitude, *Spurga o schiatta* (Relieve yourself or burst). Self restraint was harmful to the health. Once over her indulgence, Mamma would be completely composed, quickly recovering her irrepressible will to prevail in whatever life presented, be it *amaro* (sour) or *duce* (sweet).

Even as an old lady, Mamma defended her emotional extravagance. When my friend Jim asked her why she and I were fighting, Mamma stopped suddenly, and in her succinct way of speaking, replied, "No fight, doctor, jus' discush."

Many Southern Italian immigrants were illiterate and distrusted formal education, believing in the folk saying, "Be content to remain what your father was." But Mamma had a passionate respect for learning. For her, it was the basis of her hope for her children. She was constantly berating Franki for spending too much time reading the funnies: "*Viziu e natura/fin'alla morte dura*" (Habit and nature remain until you're dead). And she would ask him, "You wanna work wid a pick-a-shov all your life? Be a *zappaturu*?" Hard work may have been the answer to all life's problems, but, for Mamma, it was not the hard work of a menial job she wanted for us.

Mamma disapproved fiercely of Franki's friends whom she insisted were taking him away from his studies. When they arrived, she made them wait in the front porch. When Helvi L. wanted me to go out, she also had to wait until I finished practising my piano. And yet whenever Mamma felt that I was reading too much she would scold me with the warning that it would drive me *pazza* (crazy), a traditional Calabrese belief.

"To get ahead" was Mamma's great ambition. "What do you want to be?" was a question Mamma asked each of us continually. "A teacher" was my constant answer. "A banker" was Alfred's. Rita and Mary wanted to be nurses. Franki did not know what he wanted to be. So anxious was Mamma for our education that in 1938 she returned the Marconi radio which Daddy had bought, because the boys were listening to the boxing matches instead of doing their homework.

As a parent, Mamma encouraged no close familiarity with her children. She never took time to listen to us and was not interested in idle chit-chat. If we were frustrated, angry or fearful, she showed no concern for our emotions. We never brought home our problems from school or play. They would have been termed *cose senza significato* (things without consequence). We never asked questions, and Mamma gave us no hugs or kisses. Although we desired her approval and even worked hard for it, she extended no praise. Reared in the dour fatalism of Southern Italy, she was always guarded about life. To feel optimistic, to anticipate happiness, would surely have brought bad luck.

Mamma was by no means the *Mamma mia* of the television ads — jolly, naive and round. She defied all stereotypes.

Her kitchen was her domain. It was the largest room in our house, and throbbed with activity the whole day long. All life centred there. Though large, its furnishings were sparse: a table covered with an oilcloth, hard chairs, a cushionless rocking chair, a sink with a mirror above it and a combination cook stove. A naked light bulb hung from the centre of the ceiling. All my memories of the kitchen involve Mamma at work busy by the stove or the sink or in her rocking chair where she did her sewing and patching. We ate, played and did our homework on the kitchen table. Daddy read the newspaper aloud there. The north whitewashed wall by the table was used as a chalkboard where we did our arithmetic exercises. On the south side, a large pantry had a trap door that led to the basement where the coal furnace and expansive cupboards were located. Every night for years, until Mamma could no longer control us, we knelt in a semi-circle by her rocking chair in front of the stove and we prayed. A religious calendar hung on the door to the back porch, and a large crucifix was hooked to a nail on the wall above the entrance to the dining room.

A round oak table and chairs, an ornate mahogany buffet and a Gramophone stood in the dining room. I loved to look at the stuffed green bird adorned with coloured sequins and beads which hung from one of the ledges of the buffet. In the north-west corner, a deep closet under the stairs housed one-hundred-pound bags of sugar and flour. Our Christmas tree always stood in the south-west corner. Only during the Christmas season did we eat at the dining room table.

The parlour whose front windows looked out on a glassed-in porch held a piano and a three-piece brown leather sofa set with heavy mahogany arms. Mamma expected furniture to last forever, and we kids had to take good care of it. I polished the furniture every Saturday with lemon oil. Once a teacher friend of mine told me that she had stained her dress on one of our dining room chairs. I did not tell Mamma. We never sat in this room as a family except when special visitors came. On these occasions Rita would sing Italian songs such as "La Spagnola" or "Ciribiribin" to my piano accompaniment.

A tall mahogany wardrobe graced the north wall of the front hall. A telephone hung on the west wall. It was the only telephone in the immediate vicinity and one neighbour after another would invariably come in at lunch time to use it. We never locked our doors, and one morning we got up to find a strange man who had been drunk stretched out on the sofa; he had entered the wrong house.

Upstairs, Daddy and Mamma slept in a room that extended from one side of the house to the other. The room had a double brass bed stacked with two mattresses, a bureau covered with an assortment of sacred relics, a picture of St. Anthony in an oval frame, a votive light that Mamma lit every day, and a large metal trunk covered with a flowered throw. The sewing machine, a nut brown Singer with golden scrolls painted along the black arm had two tiers of little drawers filled with all sorts of sewing accessories. It was a bright room that got the afternoon sun. When Mamma wasn't in the kitchen, she was in her bedroom at her sewing machine or making her bed. She was fastidious about pressing out wrinkles and ridges in the bedclothes. In the Old Country, so important was the matrimonial bed to Calabrese women that they thought nothing of spending half an hour smoothing out the mattress of corn husks. Once Mamma had arranged her bed to her satisfaction, I was never allowed to sit on it.

Mamma kept a large chamber pot under her bed, and kept her money in a knotted handkerchief under the bottom of the mattress. When my sister Rita and I went to Fort Lauderdale, we put two fifty-dollar bills under our hotel mattress for safe-keeping as we had seen Mamma do. When we returned from the beach, to our horror, they were gone. We were too intimidated to say anything to the hotel management.

Above Mamma's bed hung a brightly coloured print of the Blessed Virgin Mary on her death-bed, flanked by two enormous angels to escort her to Heaven (a depiction of the Assumption, celebrated on August 15, an important holy day in Calabria). It was set in an ornate golden frame. A much smaller print of St. Barbara standing by a castle tower with a crown on her head, a sword in her right hand, and a palm branch on her left, hung on another wall.

My sisters and I shared a three-quarter metal bed in the south bedroom which was bare except for a small chest of drawers. The boys slept above the kitchen in another bare room which was divided in two just before the second world war.

A closed-in verandah extended across the front of the house, and a small porch protected the back-door entrance. The clothesline came into the porch through a narrow elongated door.

Monday was always wash day, and Mamma prided herself on being the first in the neighbourhood to have her washing out on the line. To achieve this dubious honour, she heeded the Calabrese saying: *Chi vo gapare il suo vicino si curca presto e si leva immattina* (Whoever wishes to beat his neighbour goes to bed early and rises early). Even in the depths of winter, she always hung out the clothes. Her fingers were never numb as she struggled with the stiffened laundry, which she would later drape, piece by piece, over chairs, filling the kitchen with freshly chilled air. Tuesday was ironing day, and Mamma ironed everything, even the sheets, pillow cases and tea towels, on an ironing board propped across the backs of two kitchen chairs.

Houses were not insulated in those days, and hand-stoked coal furnaces produced inconsistent heat. During the long northern winters our two-storey, eight-room house was drafty. The thick frost gathered around doors and baseboards and covered the windowpanes. I remember scraping pictures of trees, apples and stars in the thick frost of the kitchen and bedroom windows. My bed was piled so thickly with heavy blankets that I could barely turn over during the night. I dressed and undressed under the blankets between the flannelette sheets. How I hated to get up in the morning and to put my feet on the cold, cold floor.

As a skinny little girl, I used to stand on the hot air-grate in the kitchen to keep warm. Mamma and Daddy never complained of the cold. The bracing air seemed to energize Mamma who enjoyed going out on clear cold days, dressed in her black Hudson Seal coat and muff and buckled overshoes.

At that air-grate I heard some strange things being discussed at the kitchen table. It was there, for instance, that I first heard the expression *blacco enze* (The Black Hand) spoken in furtive whispers. I asked no questions, but have since discovered that the Black Hand referred to the gangs of extortionists which operated in North America. I never once heard the word *Mafia*.

During the Depression, I heard the name R.B.Bennett, *u primo ministro* and discussions of the relief camps where men worked for five dollars a month. I heard about Primo Carnera, the Italian heavyweight boxing champion, and Franceschini, an Italian immigrant who actually owned Dufferin Paving Company for which Daddy worked several summers.

From the day Mamma arrived in the New World, she wanted to speak English perfectly, and she made a serious effort to learn. But

English was not a language pronounced phonetically. She found the pronunciation and spelling of English words confusing. *Bough* was pronounced differently from *cough* or *through*, and yet they ended in the same four letters. In time, she bought a book, *Nuovissima Grammatica Accelerata Italiana-Inglese ed Enciclopedia Popolare*, by A. DeGaudenzi. Besides an Italian-English vocabulary, the book contained model letters in English and Italian for contractors and labourers and snippets of dialogue for special occasions — "at the post office," "on the train," etc. It also offered a large assortment of love letters ranging in scope from "ardent love" and "jealousy" to "a marriage proposal." Since the book was written for American citizenship and commerce, much of it was of no use to Mamma, but she referred to it throughout her life. I have it now, thumbed and worn, held together by strips of white adhesive tape.

Some immigrants had more trouble than Mamma with the language. Once a woman and her three-year-old daughter were supposed to get off the train at Fort William. The woman thought she was getting off at a place which she pronounced "For-e-villia." When the conductor announced "Fort William," she did not get off. It was only when he made his rounds for tickets after they had left Fort William that he realized his two passengers had missed their stop. He let them off at the tiny hamlet of Murillo, twenty miles further down the line.

Here, unable to speak English, frightened and exhausted, they just sat in the waiting room until a railroad employee spotted them and managed to get them on the next train back to Fort William.

After World War II when English-for-New-Canadian classes started, Mamma went to "night school" to learn English. She had a large English vocabulary but never mastered the spelling or pronunciation of English words. When I went overseas she wrote letters to me in a phonetic spelling according to her own pronunciation. I read them aloud to hear what she wrote. All her life she regretted her difficulties with English. I tried to assure her that even her idiosyncratic English was better than any of the other Italian women of her generation.

Mamma was not a talkative woman, but she liked to reminisce, in snippets, about her life in Calabria. Whenever she mentioned her little hometown, Piane Crati, a wistful yearning would come over her and she would repeat the Calabrese expression: *"Paesello mio, focolarillo mio"* (My little town, my little hearth). She told me four stories time and time again. She would recall that as a child, she had helped pick the building stones for the family *"palazzo"* — a large tall house of solid stone and thick walls built on the main road, right across from the public water fountain and the Church of St. Barbara, named in honour of the patron saint of the town. She also recalled her first day at school when she became teacher's pet: "Who is the Queen of Italy?" her teacher asked. Mamma's hand quickly went up. No other hand was raised. "Well, who is it, Siscarella?" (The Calabrese love diminutives.)

"La Regina Elena," was Mamma's eager reply.

"You see that didn't require too much thought," the teacher admonished the class. Mamma loved school.

The third recollection would always sadden her. Every year, as long as Mamma could remember, on the feast day of St. Barbara, her father had led the parade. Processions were an important part of the religious celebrations, which in the remote rural towns of Calabria offered the major excitement of the year. Marching to the music of the town band, her father threw, twirled, and flipped a twenty-foot, three-inch wide pole in the air balancing and launching it from his chin, his nose, his forehead, his shoulders and hands. The spectators who lined the route or watched from windows or balconies were invariably thrilled. He never once failed to balance and catch the *stinardu* (standard) — until parade day on December 4, 1916 when his skills began to fail him. For him, this was a sign of his impending death. "Agata, my end is near," he told his wife. He died several months later as he predicted.

But it was the fourth anecdote I love best, partly because it was about my grandmother Serafina after whom I was named. During World War I she had boarded a train alone, en route to Sicily, where two of her sons were recuperating in a military hospital. Carrying only some bread and cheese tied in a tea towel, she got as far as Palermo. There, a conductor asked her for her ticket. She had none. "You are demanding a ticket from a mother of four sons who are fighting in this war. What insolence! Two of my sons are injured. I'm going to see them. I have no ticket!" But the conductor insisted she produce a ticket or get off the train. In a burst of righteous indignation, she slapped the conductor's face.

Mamma had "special affection," to use her words, for the British monarchy. Whether she saw herself built like the Queen Mother, I don't know. But she was always fascinated by the beautiful consort of King George VI and followed her activities whenever they were reported in the newspapers. Mamma's little group of friends, Emma Fero, Rosina D'Ambrosio, Giovanina Cava, Theresina Baccari and Chichina Gallucci, which met once a month for coffee and conviviality, even called themselves "The Queen Elizabeth Club." And when King George VI and Queen Elizabeth stopped in Port Arthur on May 23, 1939, nobody could have been more excited than Mamma. She walked up to the Port Arthur Collegiate Institute to be on the route of the Royal Tour, and to catch a glimpse of her beloved Queen. Like many other Canadians of the time she loved the pomp and ceremony of British royalty.

In the Spring of 1943, Mamma was asked to pour tea at a function put on by the Women's Conservative Association of Port Arthur to honour Fiorenza D'Arneiro Johnson, the Italian-born wife of the Conservative leader of Ontario, and future premier, George Alexander Drew. Mamma was honoured and delighted, although, because it was war time, some members of the local "English" society undoubtedly found it repugnant that the invitation should have gone to an immigrant, a foreigner, an "enemy alien." Like her English hosts, she was wearing white gloves and a hat. I accompanied her to the event held in the Provincial Room of the Prince Arthur Hotel, and can still see her sitting erect and tall, officiating at one end of the long elegant tea table that glowed with its sterling and candelabras. I was so proud of Mamma, especially when she conversed with Mrs. Drew in the high Italian she had learned in school.

On the way home, however, I noticed that she wasn't happy. But she said nothing. It wasn't until several months later that she told me she had spilled some tea on the tablecloth. But it was not her fault, she was quick to point out. A woman had bumped her hand while she was pouring. I tried to diminish her shame by assuring her that few people had noticed the spill. I had not.

But it was not just the spill that bothered her. It was also the suspicion that the bump might have been a deliberate act to humiliate her. Mamma was a proud woman. For her — a Calabrese woman — *fare la bella figura* (to make a good impression) was practically sacrosanct.

4
Daddy

Daddy was a plain working man with simple habits and simple pleasures. He was stocky, sturdy and smooth-shaven, with soft grey eyes, a ruddy complexion and a bald head. He wore long fleece-lined underwear winter and summer, and he always wore suspenders. He carried his pocket watch on a heavy gold chain that extended across his chest. He was never without his Swiss Army knife with its many blades.

He could often be found playing cards at the Italian Hall on Algoma Street. He loved playing so much that Mamma would send Mary to remind him it was dinner time. Mary enjoyed being sent because Daddy was such a good player that he always had his pockets full of Hershey bars which were the stakes the married men played for.

His home was his castle. It was there, as youngsters, Rita and Mary hailed him with delight when he came home from work, hugging and kissing him, as he took off his red plaid Mackinaw and his muddy boots. They would bring him his slippers and rummage through his lunch pail for the goodies that he always saved for them. They shouted with glee when he played "Eeny, meeny, miney moe/Catch a nigger by the toe./ If he hollers let him go./ Eeny, meeny, miney moe" (I'm sure Daddy was not aware of the racism inherent in the game).

Home was where he whistled, sang, danced, played Solitaire and scanned the captions of the local paper. Home was where Daddy relaxed in the kitchen and smoked away the time. He was a chain-smoker who would cut his cigars in two and smoke half at a time. A haze of smoke encircled him, and the strong aroma of Marco Gallo tobacco permeated the house. He always kept wooden matches in his vest pocket and would strike one against his trousers with a quick clean stroke of his arm and get a light every time.

If he wasn't smoking, Daddy would chew a piece of moist tobacco cut from his plug, or he would keep a big wad of Copenhagen snuff lumped in his lower lip or in one cheek. Since we didn't have a spittoon in the house he would spit in the sink. On the job he worked with explosives, and the snuff kept his mouth moist, as well as compensating for his nicotine addiction and eliminating any fear of an explosion that might be triggered by a cigar.

Music too gave Daddy pleasure. When he was home he would turn the hand-crank of our wind-up Gramophone and take his favourite records out of the machine's red velvet compartments. His favourites were Enrico Caruso's "Vesti la giubba," Amelita Galli-Curci's "Caro Nome," and John McCormack's

"Ave Maria." My favourite was "It's Three O'clock in the Morning."

Daddy could be as merry as the tunes he sang and whistled. He regaled us with snatches of arias from Italian opera, Neapolitan songs, fragments of songs on the hit parade, and even Finnish phrases and numbers: "La Donna è mobile," "Libiamo, libiamo," "O Sole Mio," "Santa Lucia." For Mary alone, Daddy would start out in his singular sweetness of tone, "O Marie, Quanto sono perduto per te!/ Fammi dormi./ O Marie!" For Mamma, with a melting sensuality, "Mamma, mamma/ solo per te/ la mia canzone vola." And then he would break into the brisk rhythms of "La luna mezzu o mare" or into the soft, slow beats of the Scottish ditty:

jus a wee doch an doris
jus a wee drop that's a
jus a wee doch an doris
before we go awa.

It was during times like these that Daddy became ten feet tall in my eyes. I marvelled at his grace and charm. For Alfred and Franki, Daddy would count to a hundred in Finnish and repeat all the Finnish phrases and sentences he knew, except the profanities. Those we learned on Bay Street. He never finished a song or a whistled tune, claiming that his throat had started to bother him or he could not remember the words.

When the girls got older, he would swoop us into his arms and whirl us to the rhythms of a dance tune that he would sing or whistle. We loved to dance with him even in public because he was so smooth. I can still remember waltzing with him to "Now Is the Hour." Mamma would sit in the background and watch. Daddy would politely take her as a partner at least once during the evening. She was awkward, and it was only Daddy's consummate skill that made her a dancer at all.

In spite of her inability, she liked to dance the Tarantella, the traditional Southern Italian folk dance. With hands on her Calabrese hips, she kicked her feet back and forth circling around her partner. Then she would throw her hands high above her head, beating them to the dance's earthy rhythm. This ancient ritual to cure the poisonous bite of tarantula spiders was high-spirited. Mamma's version was less energetic.

Daddy was one of the few Italian men in Port Arthur who owned a car. He loved to drive. His first car was a Graham Paige. I don't remember it, but I do remember his Ford V8. It was reserved for week-ends when he would drive the family berry-picking or for picnics to Current River Park, Boulevard Lake, Wild Goose or Chippewa Park. On the way, as we sat in the back seat, we loved to sing rounds like "Three Blind Mice" and "Frère Jacques." In later years we sang "All the Nice Girls Love a

Sailor" and "Bell-Bottom Trousers" because Alfred was in the Navy.

For several years, Daddy drove us to the annual Italian picnic held at any of a number of locales around town. The boys' potato sack and wheelbarrow races, the "married ladies only" race, the ladies' nail driving contest and the egg and spoon relays were fun to watch. Alfred always won the greased pole climb. I always won the hop, step and jump race and Rita and I, the three-legged race. I remember cheering Daddy at horseshoes, and jumping and clapping when our side won the tug-of-war which would end the day's activities.

When I was eleven or so the boys won jack knives at the picnic. On the way home they were whittling on a stick in the back of Daddy's dumptruck, and one of them (I can't remember who) accidentally slashed my right hand. Blood gushed out. I did not scream because I didn't want to alert Mamma and Daddy in the cab. I put my left hand over the dripping cut and held it tightly in order to stop the bleeding. I knew that if I made a fuss the boys would get a beating. Mamma did not take me to the doctor, but bandaged the cut herself. The crescent-shaped scar can still be seen.

In the Southern Italian family, the father had the right and duty to punish any member who misbehaved or disobeyed him. Daddy, however, took no responsibility for our upbringing. Most of the time he seemed oblivious to our mischief. But when he responded to it

— the response depending more on his mood than the gravity of the offense — he enforced his authority by violence, cuffing and sometimes kicking the boys. On occasion he would explode into rage. Once he made Alfred and Franki go down to the basement where he beat them with his razor strop. The girls huddled silently upstairs in the kitchen, while Mamma, wailing and screaming, begged Daddy to stop and even tried to intervene, accidentally getting hit herself. This must have happened when a group of boys, including Alfred and Franki, broke twenty basement windows at Bay Street United Church. Every boy was sent to the police station. Within two hours Mamma had paid her sons' portion of the restitution bill. Despite this crisis, Alfred and Franki were not late for their papers that day.

I can't remember how many times Daddy strapped us girls for being noisy when we went to bed. Because there were so many blankets we felt nothing. But we did try to suppress our giggles and to talk in subdued whispers after every thrashing. Mamma disapproved of Daddy's violence. She told me that once when I was a baby, I was crying so hard that he lost patience with me and threw me across the bedroom. After Daddy's death she quietly confessed that it wasn't across the room but across the bed.

Even as a young teacher, I was the brunt of his hot temper. In December of my second year teaching, I was preparing to return to my school to stage the Christmas Concert when Daddy and I had an argument. He flew into a rage and slapped me. My glasses broke. The Christmas Concert was to start in an hour. Luckily my optometrist was at home. Even the comments of the audience that it was the best Christmas Concert ever staged at the school, even the enthusiasm of the students and the ten-dollar War Savings Certificate the School Board gave me, could not lift my spirits.

On another occasion, many years later, Daddy threw out boxes and boxes of my memorabilia that were stored in our attic. I was devastated, because they represented a lifetime of precious memories: my photographs, year books, dance cards, and letters, as well as special pieces of work my students had done over the years, including a splendid banner: *A new word each day brings good English our way.* Mamma had tried to stop him. Only her pleas kept me from leaving home.

And yet Daddy was normally warm-hearted and generous. When I was born he bought me the most expensive and fashionable articles of furniture: a wicker carriage, a wooden cradle and sleigh. The carriage sported a sliding hood with a big round window on each side and a front brake.

When Rita was five years old she got Scarlet Fever, and had to be taken to the Isolation Hospital. A large white placard on which *Scarlet Fever* was printed in bold red letters was nailed on the front wall of our house. We were all numb. Daddy cried because his beautiful blue-eyed daughter was very sick. Getting an infectious disease was a common danger then. In our family we all got chicken pox and measles and several kids at school contracted mumps and diphtheria. "Quarantine" and "isolation" were two new words for me. I didn't like their sounds or their meanings.

It was Daddy who plucked the twigs of lilacs from our two bushes in the front yard to adorn my baby brother's little white casket. Mamma never liked talking about the baby who died — Johnny, as Daddy called him. But I liked to display his photo on the dining room buffet — a photo that had come, "compliments" of the funeral director. He looked so beautiful.

It was always Daddy who bought us treats. It was he who bought Mary a bicycle — not a girl's but a boy's bike with a cross-bar. When I was eighteen, he taught me to drive his Ford V8. I recall putting my foot on the accelerator instead of the brakes and the car hitting a boulder. Mary who was sitting in the back damaged her teeth. But Daddy did not even scold me. And it was he who, for two years, gave me his car to drive back and forth to Five Mile School while he rode to work on his bicycle.

Daddy had no formal education in Italian or English. He taught himself to read and write in Italian and functioned well enough in English to do his job. He had an intuitive knack for numbers, for mental arithmetic and could invariably tell the construction engineer on a job site just how many cubic feet of gravel were needed to pave a road or make concrete for a bridge. I recall that when Daddy and Mamma visited me in France while I was teaching there, Daddy mentally calculated the exchange of dollars into francs before I had it figured out on paper.

I do not know how well he read and wrote Italian. He did not read Mamma's prayer books or the religious magazines that came from Italy. There was one book, however, that he kept looking at — an Italian classic, popular in his day, *I Reali di Francia*, a romance about the heroic deeds of Charlemagne and of his twelve great paladins in their struggles against the infidels. I still have the book, held together by black thread, its pages tattered and dog-eared and its hard cover so worn that the title is barely visible.

Daddy established a reputation as a first-rate rock foreman. He had learned his trade from years of on-site experience. His *Blasters' Handbook*, describing practical methods of using explosives, published by Canadian Industries Limited, looks as if it has not been read. Daddy never did read English well enough to understand a highly technical manual. Yet he excelled in the use of explosives, was well-known and respected for his work. So skilled was he, in fact, that the great C.D. Howe asked Daddy to accompany him to Fort William to view a demolition problem. Howe needed a large brick smokestack removed to make way for a new structure he was designing, and he and Daddy travelled to the site by streetcar. Daddy assured Howe that he could demolish the stack without damaging surrounding structures. And working by himself he did.

When the prestigious Whalen building in Port Arthur was constructed, only half the basement was excavated; the remainder was left as solid bedrock. Many years later, the Port Arthur Public Utilities Commission asked Louie — Daddy's English name at work — if he could excavate the remaining rock to basement depth so that they could install an Iron Fireman furnace. It was a delicate job because the finished half of the basement, where the PUC operated a meter repair and maintenance shop, was full of racks of kilowatt-hour meters. The PUC offered to remove the meters to prevent damage from explosions, but Daddy said he could do the job without damage. He set off the explosives so expertly that no one felt a tremor; not a window was broken.

Construction work was seasonal, but when spring came Daddy was always able to find a job, often going to isolated work sites and tiny settlements scattered throughout the boreal forest of Northern Ontario. He was accustomed to the deprivation of camp life. He did not mind the isolation, the poor food, or poor sanitation. Sleeping in windowless boxcars or ramshackle bunkhouses did not bother him. But the pesky mosquitoes and blackflies did — terribly. Never in his wildest dreams had he envisioned such torture, with no possibility of escape, defence or endurance. No wonder he adamantly refused to buy a summer "camp" as a cottage is called in Northern Ontario.

During the Depression he became a foreman on the construction of the Trans-Canada Highway. I have a vague recollection of an editorial in the local paper complaining of foreigners holding jobs while returned World War I servicemen went unemployed. There were whispers around the kitchen table that the article referred to Daddy, although it did not mention his name. Daddy lost his job.

He was first and foremost a company man whose goal was the Company's. Company time was sacrosanct. He even filled his time-keeping book at home each night so as not to waste minutes on the job. His Italian labourers called him *u caporale* or *u bosso*. He was a tough supervisor, but his reputation as a boss who did not expect his gang to work any harder than he did became legend. Louie was so well liked that this little verse about him soon circulated:

Pork and beans for the working man
Ham and eggs for Louie the foreman.

He was not identified with the macaroni and meatballs of Italian cuisine but with the camp food of the English-owned construction companies. His bosses liked him. Many of them came to our house to discuss work with him.

A.J. Isbester, District Engineer for the Ontario Government's Department of Northern Development, came often.

I remember with the most sickening vividness the time Daddy and Franki saved the west wall of the "block" from collapsing. A basement for an addition to the block was being excavated, and heavy rains that had been pouring steadily for several days were undermining the footing. The brick wall was in danger of collapsing. For an hour, inside my friend's car, I watched helplessly as my middle-aged father and young brother dug desperately to divert the water and shore up the wall. They worked the whole night through. I had never, nor have I since, witnessed such herculean labour as I did on that autumn night in 1951.

Road construction companies were not too concerned with safety measures back then; injury and death on the job were common. Daddy worked with the constant threat of cave-ins and the unpredictable nature of certain rock formations. He was seriously injured in three accidents. I must have been about seven when we received word by phone that Daddy had been injured in a dynamite blast at Wolf River, about forty miles east of Thunder Bay.

On the second occasion, Halloween 1936, Alfred and Franki, who were selling their newspapers, rushed to the waterfront because of a commotion there, only to discover that it was their father who was being put in an ambulance. He had been working on the breakwater, and the icebreaker crushed his chest against the breakwater wall. Straining with superhuman courage, Daddy tried to hold back the icebreaker with his bare hands. He was critically hurt and not expected to live. We did not have the heart to go "trick or treating". To this day the Covello children remember that they were all dressed up in their costumes and ready to leave when their father John, Daddy's cousin, announced that, out of respect, they could not go out that night.

The third accident occurred again in late Autumn when I was teaching High School in Chapleau. I felt a sudden urge to phone home and discovered that Daddy once again had been seriously injured. A dumptruck had crushed his hip. I visited him regularly in the hospital during the Christmas holidays, and he was always cheerful. He was the "darling" of Room 303, suffering pain in silence, as usual.

In Mamma, these experiences brought out the pessimism that is so embedded in the psyche of the Calabrese. With every phone call, she came to expect disaster. Her fear infected me. Every time the phone rang I, too, was afraid of bad news.

I always admired Daddy's resilience, his wonderful ability to bounce back. Never did I hear him grumble or wallow in self-pity. He took delight in his simple habits, whether it was soaking his feet in a basin of warm water and epsom salts, sharpening his straight razor on a stone, splashing Aqua Velva lotion on his face, blowing smoke rings in the air, or paring the skin off an apple in one long even strip. His was an expansive, happy nature with no pettiness, jealousy or suspicion. He did not even harbour any resentment towards the partners who had cheated him.

Coming to Canada at such a young age, he had absorbed the spirit and ideas of the New World. He was not like Mamma who was constantly quoting a Calabrese proverb to instill in us her value system. Daddy said nothing, just left us to our own devices, to nourish our own interests and ambitions. He gave us the same personal freedom he had demanded for himself as a youngster.

Unlike Mamma, he never reminisced about his childhood in Calabria. And yet, he wrote his mother faithfully, and regularly sent her substantial sums of money. Rolls of receipts survive, attesting to his generosity.

He would occasionally make proud reference to his brother, Giovanni, who had his ear cut off during World War I by an enemy sniper at Trieste. Younger than Daddy by two years, Giovanni was in the Italian King's own guard — the *Maresciallo Maggiore Comando delle Divisione di Fanteria* "Granatieri di Sardegna."

For me, the word, *Maresciallo*, conjured up the image of a handsome officer resplendent in uniform. When I visited my uncle in Rome, in 1952, he was retired from the army. He looked like Daddy and took great pride showing me his badges, his epaulettes, medals and swords. General McArthur's words came to mind: "Old soldiers never die, they just fade away."

Not only was Daddy silent about his childhood in Calabria, he said nothing about his early Canadian experiences, the hardships, sacrifices or indignities suffered. And he never spoke about his feelings.

When he did talk, his English was sprinkled with images he acquired not from the Old World he left behind but from the New World. Whenever he wished to illustrate the ultimate in authority, he would use "the King of England" for his comparison. And when he wished to express his high hopes for Port Arthur he would invariably compare it to Chicago.

Like Sir Wilfred Laurier, who predicted that the Twin Cities would become the "Chicago of the North" when he turned the first sod for the Grand Trunk Pacific Railway in Fort William in 1905, Daddy, too, had great hopes for the city where his children were born.

When I was a child, Chicago was just the name of a city where Uncle Peter, Mamma's brother, lived. At school, I learned that Chicago was "Queen of the West." It epitomized rapid development and limitless energy, the potential of the new industrial age of the nineteenth century. Many years afterwards, when I was teaching in France and visited the American Pavilion at the Brussels Fair of 1957, the Americans used Chicago to showcase to the world the phenomenal progress of the United States of America.

I was enough of Daddy's daughter that when I was interviewed in 1959 by the Assistant Director of Teacher Education for Ontario, for a position in the newly-opened Lakehead Teachers' College in Port Arthur, I was asked how I would teach Wordsworth's "The Daffodils." I replied that in my hometown it would be more appropriate to teach a poem like Sandburg's "Chicago":

> . . . *Stacker of wheat,*
> *Player with Railroads and the Nation's Freight Handler;*
> *Stormy, husky, brawling,*
> *City of the Big Shoulders:*
> . . . *Come and show me another city with lifted head singing so proud*
> *to be alive and coarse and strong and cunning . . .*

Fierce as a dog with tongue lapping for action, cunning . . . as a savage pitted against the wilderness,

> *Bareheaded,*
> *Shoveling,*
> *Wrecking,*
> *Planning,*
> *Building, breaking, rebuilding . . .*

Bragging and laughing that under his wrist is the pulse, and under his ribs the heart of the people,

Laughing!
Laughing the stormy, husky, brawling laughter of Youth . . .

Although the Lakehead never did achieve the prominence of Chicago, Daddy's pride in his adopted city lingered a lifetime.

When he returned to Calabria in 1957, after an absence of forty-five years, he discovered that he felt no attachment to his *paesello* (little town). The youth, who had resolutely refused his mother's pleas to remain in the land of his birth, had become wholly Canadian.

5
The Neighbourhood

A foot policeman always stood at the busy intersection of Bay and Algoma Streets, just a block from where we lived on Secord Street in the south end of Port Arthur. The south end was supposed to be the tough area of the city because "foreigners," as the non-English speaking immigrants were called, lived there. But we kids roamed the neighbourhood, unsupervised, and oblivious to any possible danger. Doors were never locked at night and our mothers never worried as to our whereabouts.

It was a working-class district where the modest houses were close together on long narrow lots. The majority of them were single family dwellings and privately owned. It was a stable neighbourhood, whose inhabitants were concerned primarily with the problems of economic survival.

The area throbbed with activity. Bay Street had its Finnish Labour Temple, the small Finn Hall, Maclean's Grocery Store, a Chinese hand laundry, John Wieden's Taxi, Bay Street United Church, a barber shop and pool rooms. I remember the smell of the fresh sawdust on the floor of Cut Rate Meat Market and the smell of new leather in Joe Holomego's shoe repair shop. Every summer, a group of gypsies pitched their tents in a vacant lot on Bay Street east of Algoma. Algoma Street meant Peanut Jim's Confectionery, Nyman's Drug Store, Salo's Jewellery Store, Estelle's Beauty Parlour, the International Co-operative, several cafés, shoe repair shops and lumber yards. And I remember the smell of varnish, shellac and turpentine in the huge Barton & Fisher Hardware directly behind our house. The Main Line streetcar rattled on its tracks along Algoma Street. Cornwall School marked our southern boundary. And although the automobile was taking over during the 1930s, horses were still delivering our bread and milk. And there was a constant stream of people walking — mothers carrying bundles to and from the shops; fathers carrying lunch-pails to and from work; children carrying books to and from school; young boys and girls walking up and down with no destination in mind; and men, smoking and talking in Finn, slouching along the walls of the big Finn Hall and the small Finn Hall which was "Communist," a word we whispered because it was supposed to be "bad" although we did not know why.

Our family of five children was the largest on the block. As a result, I was often the butt of jokes and afraid that there might be another baby to increase the number. My cousin, Theresa C., remembers that her older sister Rosalie used to pay her sisters and brothers ten cents each to duck down in their dad's car whenever he was driving through St. Patrick's Square so that her friends would not know there were so many children in the family. In those days large families were always associated with Italians and Catholics.

Our neighbours were of various national origins: Finnish, Swedish, Scottish and English. Most of the fathers were lumberjacks, carpenters or commercial fishermen — seasonal workmen who, like Daddy, worked out of town. Many of the Finnish mothers took in one or two roomers. There was only one other Italian family, the G's, who had a son whom we kids thought was "crazy." Reputed to have great strength, he roamed the neighbourhood followed by kids who made fun of him and called him "Giggle-lee-gee Giggle-lee-gee" because he never spoke. His boots were the biggest I had ever seen.

Each family jealously guarded its privacy. Beyond a brief exchange of greetings, Mamma and her neighbours — Mrs. Happonen, Mrs. Hyrvanen, Mrs. Neale, Mrs. Halonen, Mrs. Nykanen, Mrs. Williams, Mrs. Lindbergh — rarely engaged in conversation, and Mamma had very little to do with them. With their limited vocabularies, no commonality of experience or language, and the heavy work demands of their families, there was only time for a smile. Neighbours lived their own lives and did not intrude upon one another. I never knew the first names of the mothers in the neighbourhood. I seldom spoke to them. They had thick accents and spoke broken English like my mother. I do not recall ever meeting, let alone talking to, a neighbourhood father.

If no social interaction and little neighbourly feeling existed among our parents, there was friendly familiarity among us children. Although we Petrones were the only kids on the block who went to a Catholic school, we played together throughout the neighbourhood. Our religion identified us more than our ethnic roots, although we called each other ethnic names — Polock, Bohunk, Wop, Finnlander — sometimes in jest and sometimes to sting.

As a young girl, I did not form any bosom relationships. I had no "best friend," and I was seldom invited inside another girl's home. Pajama parties were unheard of. Kids would stand by their back doors and call each other by name to come out and play. Or kids would just meet on street corners and in the back lanes. My friends called me Sarah despite Mamma's protests that they call me by my real name.

The baptismal bond between child and godparent and their families is very strong in Calabrese society. So strong, in fact, that the baptismal relationship is referred to as *u San Giovanni* (the St.John) after the saint who had baptized Christ. This symbolic kinship possesses its own terms of address — *compare* for godfather and *comare* for godmother. It is expected to involve a high degree of mutual respect. I loved my godmother, Comare Marietta Scarnati. Once she brought me back a bracelet from a trip that she had taken to Texas.

Gli anziani (the elders) were the most revered and beloved in the hierarchical structure of the traditional Italian family. We had only one, Mamma's mother, whom we called Nanna. She was a frail, bent little woman who dressed in black and was always seated on a chair at my Aunt Maria Prezio's house. Mamma visited her regularly to comb her hair and bring her cream puffs. I never spoke to her. She seemed so austere. I was afraid of her. My Prezio cousins, however, remember her as an affectionate Nanna who would walk to the gate to greet them when they came home from school and who always had hot cocoa ready for them.

Daddy's *Zio* (Uncle) Francesco and *Zia* (Aunt) Rosaria Covello were close to us. I recall Zio Francesco well because every Easter he brought us bags of Easter eggs and bunnies. Mamma had great respect for Zio and Zia.

When we visited our relatives and Mamma's close friends, all of whom lived within walking distance, we were so well-mannered that we never stirred from Mamma's knees until she gave us permission to do so. When food was served, we would wait for Mamma's approval before we reached for anything.

Kinship and friendship were based on mutual *rispetto* (respect), frequently expressed by gift exchanges and favours rendered. To accept a gift was to create an obligation and not to fulfil an obligation was to cut a poor figure. Mamma took great care to nourish friendships and often lamented the fact that in Canada one lost friends as easily as one lost buttons.

Some of her friendships were strengthened by her being one of the very few Italian women in Port Arthur who could read and write. She wrote letters for those who were *inalfabetto* (illiterate). Mary remembers Mrs. Turco best because when she visited her, she always served Shaw's honey-dipped doughnuts.

But Mamma's English was not proficient enough for her to manage her business affairs, especially over the phone. Because there were no Italian doctors, lawyers, bank managers or clerks in the city's department stores, I became Mamma's interpreter when I was about seven years of age. I can still remember climbing a chair to reach the wall telephone.

Summer was the season I loved best, even though we did the same things year after year. My parents never made any plans. They bought us no toys, no sports equipment. Nobody organized our activities or taught us our games. We improvised and made our own fun. We were never bored.

We were lean and brown and radiated health and joy. We rolled on the grass and loved to go barefoot. There were no aluminum cans or flip tops or broken beer bottles to cut our feet. We looked for four-leaf clover in the empty lots; we held buttercups under one another's chin to test whether we liked butter.

We pulled the petals off the daisies: "He loves me, he loves me not." We crowned ourselves with dandelion chains. We played all the English games: tag, giant step and hide-and-seek. We knew all the English songs — "London Bridge Is Falling Down," "The Farmer in the Dell," "Ring Around the Rosie," "Go In and Out the Windows."

On the Barton-Fisher block and Cornwall School, there were the high fire escapes which I climbed to the very top whenever I could gather enough courage. There was the large display window at Peanut Jim's candy store to look into. There was Nyman's Drug Store which I visited every few days for free samples: small bars of soap, little tins of mentholatum or cards of ExLax tablets. There was Algoma Street where I watched the parades and American cars go by. Many American tourists came across the border at Pigeon River and into Port Arthur to buy fine English china and woollens. Every time I saw an American car I licked my right thumb and stamped it on the palm of my left hand. We kids loved to compete as to who had stamped the most cars. When I got a little older I would sit on the curb at the corner of Cumberland and Arthur Streets on Saturday nights and listen to the MacGillivray Pipe Band. To this day, I love the droning of the bagpipes. Sometimes the Salvation Army band played at the same intersection. I loved to listen to the brass, especially the trumpet. On those occasions I considered myself lucky indeed.

We played on the streets, in the back lanes, the backyards, and in the vacant lots between Holomego's Shoe Repair and Bay Street United Church. The lot next door became vacant when Mrs. Neale, our Irish neighbour, moved up the hill. I watched her whole house being transported on a huge platform pulled by a team of horses.

Every summer, for years, Alfred and Franki built a "shack" with potato sacking, bean poles, scrap lumber and tin in the only space available in the backyard, an ugly patch of ground between the house and Mamma's garden. The shack was either our library or school. I played the teacher or the librarian. I drew Union Jacks and Maple Leaves and had my little sisters colour them. I made library cards from the clean side of used paper and copied stories from the Red Primer for them to read. Paper was a great treasure, and I can still remember how rich I felt when a school chum whose father worked in the pulp mill gave me a large bundle of it in a variety of colours, pink, lime green, soft yellow and light mauve. I made it last for several years.

I developed a passion for books that started when I learned to read the Red Primer. My parents did not buy books, and there were no library books at St. Joseph's School. I can't remember where I learned about a place one could get books free. I do remember, however, my first library card. I think it was the first thing I ever felt I owned. And I was delighted.

I used to walk each Saturday to the Public Library which was housed then in the Ruttan Block on South Court Street about six blocks away. Physically, it was a drab place divided into two large high-ceilinged rooms with shelves reaching up twenty feet.

As I remember, the librarians gave me no guidance. I was not choosy. I would read anything. There was no children's section, only a few low shelves reserved for books that were "suited for children." And there were no lavishly illustrated books as there are today. Over and over I would borrow the same books from the children's shelves. I would read any book from the first page to the last whether I liked it or not. I remember reading and re-reading the animal stories of Thornton Waldo Burgess, stories about Buster Bear, Peter Cottontail and Mrs. Peter Rabbit, although they didn't have much significance for me.

It was the cartoon characters who could keep me entertained: Popeye the sailorman, his zany girlfriend Olive Oyl and his traitorous friend J. Wellington Wimpy; L'il Abner Yokem, a hill-billy from the Kentucky backwoods; the mischievous Katzenjammer kids; Joe Palooka, the naive heavyweight who won the 1931 world boxing championship; and Barney Google with the "goo-goo-googly eyes." I also liked Dick Tracy and female characters such as Little Orphan Annie and Jane Arden, newspaper reporter. We imitated their antics and their speech.

As I got older, we played with skipping ropes and balls, though I do not remember Mamma ever buying me a ball or a rope. But we shared and somehow I managed. We had an enormous repertoire of skipping and ball games. I loved their well-defined rhythms and rhymes and never tired of skipping to rhymes like these:

I am a Girl Guide
Dressed in blue
These are the actions
I can do.
Stand at attention
Bend your knees
Salute to the captain
Bow to the Queen

One, two, three
Sugar, butter, tea
I call Helvi in for tea
How many cups did she drink
One, two, three, etc. (Pepper)

Nor did I tire of bouncing a golf ball on our front walk:

Bouncy, bouncy, bally
I broke my sister's dolly
She gave me a slap
I paid her back
Bouncy, bouncy, bally.

Or throwing an India rubber ball against a brick wall while we acted out:

Plany, clapsy
Roll the pin
Tobaksi
High wall
Low wall
Touch your heel
Touch your toe
Over you go
Right hand
Left hand
Touch your heel
Touch the other
Touch them both
Touch the ground
Turn around.

As young teen-agers we played "Run Sheep Run," "Kick the Can," "Red Light" and "Red Rover." I loved jumping "Hopscotch" and playing "Peg" best. Peg was played on the street with a small piece of wood tapered to a point at each end. We would hit one end of it with a stick, flipping it in the direction of a goal. The kid who was able to put the peg in the goal first was the winner.

Girls did not play with the boys, who played in gangs: "The South End," "The Coal Docks," "Current River," "Brent Park," or "Oliver Road." The South End gang — Petrone, Agostino, Fero, Phillips — played baseball at Cornwall School and, on a sawdust field at the corner of Bay and Water Streets, touch football and rugby with no helmets and pads. Gangs in those days were unlike today's skinheads or punkers with their code of dress, hairstyles, clothing or music. They were groups of youths who lived in the same neighbourhood and played together.

The girls never ventured beyond the immediate vicinity, but the boys went everywhere. They swam in their private hole on the McIntyre River — Bare Ass Bend, they called it. They would swing on trees and jump into the pool, which they had deepened by piling up branches like beavers.

There was one girl in our block, Norma, who remained aloof and did not play with us. Norma was "English," and an only child. I learned recently that her father had a steady job on the railroad. No girl in the block ever thumbed her nose or stuck out her tongue at Norma. And not one of us dared chant: "I see London/ I see France/ I see Norma's dirty pants." We were all too much in awe of her. Norma had lots of dolls and toys and owned a tricycle. I used to watch her ride it down the sidewalk. On three or four occasions she invited me to play in her backyard. I always did what she told me because I felt so privileged just to be there. We played Tarzan. Tarzan of the Apes was the son of Lord and Lady Greystoke who had been marooned by pirates in Africa. As a baby he was carried off by a she-ape and reared in the jungle. When he was a young man he fell in love with the beautiful Jane Porter, a blonde American who had come to Africa with her professor father. Norma and

I invented our own little dramas of Tarzan rescuing the fair heroine. Norma always played Jane. I played Tarzan. I never got to be Jane.

We grew up during the hungry 1930s, the Great Depression, when able-bodied young men, "hobos," we called them, could not find work and rode the freight cars across the country. I remember them coming to our house begging for food. Mamma would ask them to come in and eat at our kitchen table until Mrs. Neale, our neighbour, advised her to stop. She was afraid they might be carrying germs which we would then spread to her children. After that, Mamma kept the hobos in the back porch to eat their food.

During the 1930s, the RCMP kept surveillance over the Red Finn Hall since it was the meeting place for Communists. Acting under a Criminal Code statute against "unlawful association," the RCMP harassed the Communist party, broke up meetings, dispersed audiences, raided party offices, confiscated literature and arrested activists. The scourge of Communism had to be erased in Canada.

We were always fascinated but scared too by the activities that took place around the Finn Halls. The Red Finn Hall was the headquarters of the IWW, the International Workers of the World, an American-based revolutionary industrial union. We kids were told that IWW stood for "I want work" or "I won't work," and I recall bringing home their leaflets and Tim Buck stickers. I did not know who Tim Buck was then, but I liked his name and in my child's mind associated him with Buck Rogers. I knew somehow that IWW literature was forbidden, and I never told Mamma that I was secretly hiding it in a buffet drawer. The words "Red" and "Communist" held a fascination for me. When I learned that our new neighbours, the Ahos, had gone to Russia, but had returned to Port Arthur, disillusioned and destitute, I regarded them with curiosity. When he was older, Alfred helped type up pamphlets for the IWW and ran them off on their Gestetner.

The Finnish Labour Temple, better known as the big Finn Hall, housed the Hoito restaurant in the basement, popular then with the bushworkers. Once Daddy took us there for supper because Mamma was sick. I recall the long bare tables and the plates filled high with food, and the smell of Finnish coffee bread and fish.

The Finlandia Club, a gymnastic organization, practised in the big Finn Hall. Somehow Alfred got to be a member. For years he practised every Sunday afternoon on the parallel bars, the "horses" and the flying rings. By the time he reached high school he was a graceful gymnast.

Mamma did not know that Alfred spent so much time at the Finn Halls. She had no interest in sports. In fact, she disapproved of them, and was angered once when Alfred was brought home with a sprained ankle from playing in a football game. Only a fool would play a game in which he could be injured. Life was harsh enough.

Alfred recalls hiding in the space between Holomego's Shoe Repair and the pool room across from the Red Finn Hall, watching several RCMP officers on horseback attempting to disperse a workers' meeting. Suddenly there was an eruption of violence, and Alfred heard a loud noise. A man had been shot. The next day funeral marchers paraded down Secord Street to the beat of drums carrying the dead man's casket on their shoulders. It was a traumatic experience for a young boy and one which would influence Alfred much later when, as a criminal lawyer, he dedicated himself to the defense of victims of police brutality.

August brought the Canadian Lakehead Exhibition. We called it the Circus, and year after year I counted down the days to its arrival. But I had to earn my nickels to go. It was difficult, but usually I would be able to raise about thirty cents, enough for the "Kiddies Day" entrance fee, one ride, one sideshow and one thing to eat. In spite of my lack of money, I was excited by the sights, sounds and smells of the midway: the snarling lions, the clanking elephant chains, the ring master's barking commands, the stirring marches, the pink candy floss, the hot dogs, buttered popcorn and candied apples. I could also get glimpses, for free, of the clowns, the magicians, the female acrobats in pink tights, and the human freaks — the midgets and fat ladies. And I could watch men testing their skill with darts or rings, handballs or rifles. Those who won would get big stuffed dolls or animals and then give them to their lady friends. It was not proper behaviour for women to compete.

I paid to ride the gaily coloured wooden horses pumping up and down the poles of the merry-go-round as the calliope piped "I'm Forever Blowing Bubbles." When I got older I rode the "Caterpillar" or "The Whip." They frightened me out of my wits but I loved it. I was always too cowardly to ride the Ferris Wheel and it wasn't until many years later when I was teaching in France that a friend of mine was finally able to get me on one.

I paid to enter the chamber of distorted mirrors or to watch the motorcyclists racing around perpendicular walls. One year I even paid to see John Dillinger's enormous black limousine.

The Canadian Lakehead Exhibition was simultaneously an agricultural fair. Local farmers showed their livestock as well as their garden and farm produce. I loved going to the home baking section where I would gaze and gaze, my mouth watering at all sorts of "English" pies, cakes, salads and, best of all, the homemade candy. Mamma was the first Italian woman in Port Arthur to enter the needlework competitions. In 1936 she won two second prizes, one for a "child-knit costume" and another for a bedspread.

Daddy's friend, George Wardrope, city alderman and later provincial cabinet minister, was, for years, the jovial master of ceremonies for the grand finale of the Exhibition. He often came to our house and was one of those special guests for whom Mamma obliged us to sing, dance and play the piano. He always looked jaunty in his white straw hat and white shoes. I can still hear his words, "round and round she goes and where she stops nobody knows," as he turned the wheel for the number of the winner of the grand prize which was always the latest model car. Also on the stage of the grandstand stood Port Arthur's popular mayor, Charlie Cox. He always wore a white suit. The Mayor knew Daddy by his first name. Imagine!

Summer in Port Arthur was always too short for me. And the winter was always too long. Winter temperatures would sometimes dip to minus 40° F. We didn't have today's thermal wear to protect us and the intense cold would drive me deep into my wool coat. My toes and fingers grew numb. Ice crystals gathered on my face. Frost bit my ears. And my glasses would steam up, so that I could not see. And then there was always the pain of thawing out as I huddled on the hot air vent in the kitchen.

Sometimes a blinding blizzard would rage, piling up the heavy snow in drifts that buried everything. Beginning at the back steps, my brothers would dig deep trenches, with sides higher than my head, so that we could get out to the street. Once, as a high-school student, I walked through a tunnel my brothers had dug, stepped carefully into the tracks that the horse-pulled sleigh wagons had made in the street, then trudged through the drifts in Waverley Park to reach the top of the hill, only to find that PACI was closed.

In spite of my struggle with the cold, I had some good times in winter. I made the snow into balls and men, forts and tunnels. I liked to watch the snowflakes fall and to listen to the crunch as I stepped on the snow's crust. Lying on my back, I would spread my arms, and flapping them, become an angel in the snow. I enjoyed snapping the dagger-like icicles from window sills and sucking the water out.

Five of us shared one sled. We took turns shooting down Bay Street Hill. One time a car almost hit me as I sped past Ontario Street. My narrow escape left me so scared I never went again.

The greatest excitement of winter was Christmas, full of joy and sacred symbolism. Not that we would receive many gifts. We never got toys or games or books from Santa. At Barton & Fisher's I would stand with my little sister in my arms in the long lines eager to sit on Santa's knee to receive a sucker. And when Santa arrived at Eaton's, I remember pulling Mary to the store in the large red sled that Daddy had bought for me when I was a baby. Holding her in my arms, I'd wait in line, slowly climbing several flights of stairs to see Santa and get another sucker.

A few days before Christmas, Alfred and Franki would go to the bush with Daddy to pick our Christmas tree. Daddy knew where to get the best spruce or balsam. Sometimes they would bring home two or three trees so that the girls could pick just the right one to fit in the corner of the dining room. The sudden smell of the fresh balsam filled the room. We would spend a whole afternoon or morning decorating the tree, each of us responsible for lights or tinsel or baubles and all of us full of a wonderful patience to make the tree perfect.

Finally, on Christmas Eve, we hung our every-day stockings on a wire that stretched behind the kitchen stove and was ordinarily used for drying clothes. I recall going to bed and listening to the sounds downstairs, trying to identify them until I dozed off to sleep. When we got up Christmas morning, we would rush downstairs eager to look into our stockings even though we knew what Santa had left. Each year it was the same: an orange, an apple, a banana, some nuts and hard candies, and a ten cent piece which was invariably used to go to the traditional Christmas Day hockey match in the Port Arthur Arena. Mamma considered gift-giving a minor part of the Christmas festivities. As she so often told us, it was the magic of the birth of baby Jesus that was important. Mamma and Daddy never exchanged gifts. As we got older we bought each other toys and games: Snakes and Ladders, Chinese Checkers, Monopoly, Pick-up Sticks, and Parcheesie. I recall one Christmas buying my little sister, Mary, a doll and a china tea set. I had never owned either but I wanted her to have them. And I also recall that my first gift to Mamma was a pretty moss-green ceramic vase that I had admired for months in Salo's, the jewellery store behind our house on Algoma Street.

The house was full of music at Christmas. The family would gather around the piano and sing one carol after another: "Silent Night," "The First Noel," "Away in a Manger" and, Mamma's favourite, "We Three Kings of Orient Are."

During the holidays, I occasionally went skating. Our neighbourhood rink was the world-famous "Milk Rink," as it came to be known, because it was flooded by the Port Arthur Co-Op Dairy from their oversupply of skim milk. It was located at the junction of Fort William Road and Memorial Avenue. Loudspeakers broadcast "The Blue Danube" or "The Skater's Waltz" or "Life in the Finland Woods." How I longed to move to the rhythm of these waltzes. But I didn't have any skates of my own. And the ones I borrowed were so big I would wobble on to the ice. Each time it was the same scene: I feared the boys who played "crack the whip." I envied the girls who danced on skates, or glided gracefully around the rink, alone or arm in arm with boys or other girls, while I looked for the safety of the boards. A pot-bellied stove heated the hut where we put on our skates. I spent most of the time by the stove in the hut.

For several years Alfred and Franki made a rink in our backyard. When they did not have a puck, they used cans or frozen horse turds — anything that would bounce, roll or slide. Hockey was Port Arthur's consuming winter sport. If the long-standing rivalry between the Twin Cities aroused lively public debate, the Christmas Day match between the Port Arthur Bearcats and the Fort William team raised the thunder of stamping feet and the clapping and roaring of thousands. When the famous Laprade brothers and Bones McCormack skated on the ice, the Port Arthur spectators leapt for joy. In 1939 when the Port Arthur Bearcats won the Allen Cup, the whole city went wild.

In 1950 we moved into a brick house on North Hill street. In 1980, when I bought my first house, I chose one on the crest of Mariday hill. From my bedroom I can look down on the old neighbourhood and the room where I was born on my parent's bed. Bay Street has now become "trendy." With its Finn shops, the Hoito Restaurant, and its ethnic food it attracts people from all over the city. Secord Street is still a clean street of neat houses, front porches and flower beds. The two lilac bushes are gone from number 147.

6
Italo-Canadese

We spoke Italo-Canadese within the family, with relatives and friends of our parents. Italo-Canadese was a special language — an amalgam of spoken dialect and working-class English that was developed by Italian immigrants in the New World. It proved to be a practical medium of communication for them.

The new idiom was unique to the immigrant — speech that was neither Italian nor English, and was as different from either language as any Italian dialect is different from standard Italian. Because each region in Italy had its own local dialect, there were many variations in the pronunciation of the idiom. My parents came from Calabria and so we spoke the *Calabrese* version. Few in Calabria — let alone in Italy — would have understood it.

Although many of the English words in the new patois had Italian equivalents, most immigrants wanted to speak English, if even with their own strange pronunciation.

Here is a sampling:

English Word	Italo-Canadese	Italian Word
car	karru	macchina
boss	bossu	capo
business	bisinisse	commercio
all right	orraitte	va bene
goodbye	gutbai	arrivederci
thank you	tenk yu	grazie
that's enough	azzonoffo	basta
what's the matter	vazzumaru	cose succede
hurry up	aireoppa	movete
how much	omaccio	per quanto

The New World, of course, introduced new concepts for which there were no Italian equivalents. The notions of girlfriend and boyfriend, for instance, were new to the Italians whose courtship system was not like that of North America. As a result, the immigrants incorporated English words into their new vocabulary. "Girlfriend" became "gellafrenda," and "boyfriend," "boiafrendu."

When I used such words, I did not know that I was speaking the immigrant idiom. In fact, I didn't find out until years later, when an older Canadian colleague, who spoke Italian, could not understand a conversation I was having with my mother. I recall her telling me that the Italian we spoke could not be the "real" Italian which, in her estimation, was so much more melodious. I was humiliated.

When Mamma became President of the Ladies Auxiliary to the Italian Benevolent Society and read to me in elegant fashion the speeches which she wrote in the "real" Italian, I understood what my cultured friend meant.

I regret that I did not learn my maternal language. Of all Italy's dialects, Calabrese is the closest to the ancient Roman, and is still rich in pure latinisms, such as *muliera* (wife) *figliola* (girl) and *tata* (father), Mamma always referred to her father as *Tata*. I also regret that I did not learn the standard Italian of Dante, Petrarch and Boccaccio.

I may have forgotten much of my Italo-Canadese, but I have not forgotten Mamma's intense desire to speak English well.

7
Food

Mamma loved to eat. She enjoyed cooking, and, like most Italian Mammas, prepared food with the utmost loving care. It was her way of showing her love for her children and friends, of celebrating in the joy and warmth that good food and company bring. Her continuous refrain "*Mangia, mangia*" (Eat, eat) still rings in my ears.

On Sundays and holidays, birthdays and feast days Mamma's cooking was unsurpassed. Every Sunday we had spaghetti and *purpette* (meatballs). I can still see Mamma, with a white tea towel wrapped around her head, turban style, making *purpette*, working the meat and the eggs, sprinkling in her favourite herbs, and handrolling the mixture into balls. A good pungent *sucu* (sauce) was essential and Mamma took special pride in hers. Before the rest of us even woke up, she would start the *sucu*, made from spareribs, tomatoes and garlic, oregano, bayleaf, basil and rosemary. By the time we were ready to go to church, a splendid aroma floated through the house from bedroom to basement. The *sucu* bubbled and simmered all day until it reached that thick rich flavour that Mamma's discriminating taste demanded.

The spareribs were so tender that they shed their meat with just the touch of a fork.

When I was older, during a public-speaking summer course at the University of Western Ontario, my professor assigned a "how to" topic. I chose the topic, "The secret is in the sauce: how to make the perfect Italian sauce." I recalled exactly how Mamma did it. Whether it was the connotative power of the words that made the sauce tantalizing to my professor, I do not know, but he gave me an A+. However, when in later years, I actually tried to make Mamma's sauce, my severest critic John would invariably say, "Well, it's not up to Luisa's."

For very special Sundays, Mamma made her own pasta rather than using the store-bought. On a large wooden kneading board (*timpagniu*) that Daddy had made for her, she would break one egg after another into a well in the centre of a mound of flour. Her capable hands then rhythmically pounded the mixture until the dough was moulded into a smooth and shiny ball. Then, with a *mannerello* (a yard long rolling pin), she would stretch out the ball of dough until it covered the large board. Next, the circle of dough was folded like a jelly roll and sliced, each slice unrolling into a long strip. These strips would be left on the board on the kitchen table or taken to the dining room table to dry for several hours. Mamma's pasta was always perfect. Just before dinner she would gather the strips of pasta, put them in a big pot of boiling water, and then drain them in the *sculapasta* (colander) that had been brought for her from Calabria. Testing with her practiced touch and taste, she knew when they had reached that *al dente* moment of perfection.

My favourite Italian meal, *stranguglia previti*, made with mashed potatoes, was a treat Mamma reserved for very very special days. Translated from the Calabrese, the words mean "strangle the priests," but in modern restaurant use, the dish is known as *gnocchi* (small potato dumplings). The Calabrese hold a historic contempt for their *sacerdoti* who, in days gone by, used to visit the peasant homes and to take away the best of their harvests. Once the dough was cut into plump thimble-sized pieces, Alfred and I would press each one in the centre with the index finger of our right hands and then arrange the pieces carefully in rows on a floured board so that they did not stick to each other. Mamma was very fussy. On the days that she made *stranguglia previti*, we kids were always on our best behaviour, not even peeking into the pots on the stove which were always under clouds of steam.

Mamma baked Calabrese pastries throughout the year — *frisine, taralli* and *mastazzole*. She made bushels of each. The *frisine*, rich little loaves of bread spiced with *anise*, were split in half with a fork after they were baked to give each half a rough surface. The halves were then put in the oven to be toasted ever so lightly. I recall dunking our *frisine* in our breakfast cocoa.

The *taralli* were flavoured with lemon, boiled in water and then baked like a bagel. My very own favourite sweet, the *mastazzole*, were made from dark honey and flour mixed to a consistency that had to be just right so as not to bake too hard. When she found time, Mamma made bread. And, oh, how my brothers and sisters enjoyed eating the dough fried in hot oil and sprinkled with sugar!

Christmas and Easter had their own traditional breads and pastries. On Palm Sunday, we ate *ginetti, i dolci delle palmi* (the sweets of the palms). They were shaped like dough-nuts that had been indented horizontally on the outer edge, baked, then dipped in a cooked eggwhite and sugar icing, and put in a warm oven to dry. Mamma's Easter breads were made from a dough that was firmer and sweeter than that used in everyday bread. They were fashioned into two shapes, one, *cuzupa*, for the girls, and another, *cuculu*, for the boys. The *cuzupa* was a round loaf and the *cuculu*, a log shape. Both were decorated with braids of dough and eggs in their shells inserted at intervals.

But it was Christmas, of all the special feast-days, that entailed the most elaborate food preparation. My mouth waters now when I think of the Christmas table of my childhood. Mamma would begin weeks in advance preparing the traditional foods. There were the baked delicacies which she made only at this time, huge batches of *turdilli* made with

Marsala, a sweet amber-coloured wine, and *scalille* made with dozens of eggs. Both were deep-fried in olive oil and then dipped in hot honey. We did not complain if our fingers burned when the hot oil in the roasting pan firecracked. For days, the smell of olive oil permeated our clothes and furniture, in fact, the whole house. I did not like the smell, but I knew what it meant and so did not complain. There were the *pitte improgliate*, too, my favourite Christmas pastry, which my godmother made to perfection. They were rolled like an English jelly roll but filled with aromatic spices — nutmeg, cinnamon, allspice and a variety of dried fruits.

The Christmas cake — acquired from the "English" — became tradition in our house too. Mamma's was legendary — very dark and packed with dried fruits, nuts, glacéed fruit and spices, then laced with brandy or rum. Mamma wrapped hers in butcher paper for storage.

Christmas was the only time of the year when Mamma and Daddy really splurged. Daddy bought cases of pop, boxes of Japanese oranges, fresh and dried fruit of every kind — bananas, grapes, pomegranates, dates and figs; all sorts of nuts — pecans, walnuts, peanuts, cashews, Brazil nuts, almonds. And always a box of *torrone*, a nougat candy, each piece in its own brightly decorated mini-box. With such wonderful things to eat, we wanted Christmas to go on forever. If it was a Christmas when our relatives in Calabria had sent us *crucette*

— baked figs stuffed with walnuts and shaped like a cross — my Christmas was complete.

Christmas Eve was a day of fast and abstinence. Dinner was always traditional, with no meat. We ate the conventional *baccala a lu furno* (dried salt codfish) which had taken days to prepare, in order to get rid of the salt and dryness. There was pasta — angels' hair in a sauce of garlic and fried anchovies — as well as all sorts of salads, olives, and *lupini* (dried beans) which had been soaked in water that was changed daily. I never acquired a taste for *lupini*, but I remember relatives and friends smacking their lips as they peeled the skins off, and cousins squirting the beans out and shooting them at each other. For feasts, like Christmas and Easter, when we served wine, Mamma would propose her toast. With a glass of wine in one hand, she would begin, "*Questo vino è bianco e fino.*" Taking an olive from a bowl she would continue, "*E io mi mangiu un'oliva.*" Then with a sweep of her arm towards everyone seated at the table, she would conclude her toast with the words, "*Facciu un brindisi a tutta la compagnia.*" And then she would drink from her glass. We, in turn, would raise our glasses and toast her and each other.

On this special night of the year, as was the Calabrese custom, the food remained on the table all night, not for Santa Claus and his reindeer, but as a symbolic feast for the Holy Babe. We children made sure to tell Santa Claus that the food was for him too — not just a snack of cookies and milk like the English kids put out but a real meal with many courses.

Christmas was the one time of the year when the dining room table was always set for guests who might drop in to wish us good health and good fortune, *Buon Natale* and *Felice Anno Nuovo*.

For the rest of the year, except on Sundays and holy days or birthdays, Mamma was a "one pot" cook, following the cuisine of Calabria which was basically peasant cooking inherited from generations of forbears. Weekday meals were usually a steaming hot *minestra* or *cassarola*, always served with a salad of *cicoria* or escarole spiced with vinegar, salt and olive oil, and eaten with big chunks of crusty Italian bread. Mamma had the traditional Calabrese reverence for bread, serving it with everything, even pasta.

For the *minestra*, Mamma would send Alfred or Mary to the corner butcher shop for "a five-cent soup bone." This, with mountains of vegetables, Mamma's favourite herbs, and potatoes or pasta for thickening, made a hearty meal for her kids.

Mamma applied her creative talents to a variety of casseroles, using potatoes or pasta as a base. There was pasta mixed with beans — navy, or pinto, black, kidney, lima or broad; pasta combined with peas or chick peas; pasta and endive; potatoes with zucchini or tomatoes.

The *taste* of the food was Mamma's constant preoccupation. She tasted all the time, savouring each bit to the fullest. She considered basting an important source of good taste. I can still see her seated by the oven basting the roast chicken or roast potatoes.

We never ate meat on Fridays or other days of abstinence. But instead of fish, which most Catholic families ate, Mamma prepared dishes such as fried potatoes and green peppers; green peppers and eggs; *frittata* — a mixture of eggs, cheese and onion; an assortment of fritters: boiled escarole or zucchini, drained, chopped and mixed with eggs, cheese and a little flour. She also liked stuffing vegetables such as eggplants and peppers. And she stewed tomatoes and potatoes with greens.

Mamma's *sauza* was delicious. She made it in a mound shape with layers of boiled zucchini and bread crumbs, and the freshest of basil doused with oil, garlic, and vinegar. She made her tomato salad out of garden-fresh tomatoes dressed with sweet onions, basil and olive oil.

Whatever fruit we had in the house was our dessert. In winter, it was always an apple. We turned the word into a sing-song chant: "A-pp-l-e, A-pp-l-e." And then one of us would be told to go into the basement to get the apples from the barrel. I cannot recall Mamma ever saying to my brothers and sisters who had hearty appetites, "You're eating too much."

Meals were the focal points of the day. They were social times filled with fun. When we got too noisy, as we often did, Mamma, and Daddy, if he were home, would call a stop. Mamma presided at the table. It was she who served us.

But Daddy's love of food — especially of watermelon and ice-cream — was just as enormous as hers. If the watermelons had not arrived in Port Arthur soon enough for him, he would drive to Grand Marais in Minnesota to have his first watermelon feast of the summer. Daddy's love of ice cream lasted a lifetime. Even as an old man he would take his grandson Michael in the big black Oldsmobile 98 with the power windows to go to the Dairy Queen.

Except for ice cream, any food that was *gelata* (frozen) was bad. If meat somehow got frozen in winter, it was thrown out. Ironically, years later, Franki would go into the frozen food business, and Mamma moved with the times.

As a young girl, I was upset with Mamma and Daddy's preoccupation with food. I wanted to be thin, not because I was worried about cholesterol — the word was not even known then — but because the most popular movie stars, my role models, Jean Harlow, Rita Hayworth, Joan Crawford, Gene Tierney, Carole Lombard, were all thin. For years, all I would have for breakfast was raw egg and milk beaten to a froth. And yet, although I avoided greasy

Italian foods, I was not concerned with fatty foods that were not considered Italian. I was ecstatic about banana splits, especially those which my sister Rita, who worked at the Port Arthur Café, made for me. Hers were huge — three big scoops of hard ice cream with mounds of whipping cream, lots of nuts, pineapple bits, and chocolate syrup flanked with strips of bananas, and topped with maraschino cherries.

Everything we ate was fresh or homemade. The only packaged foods we ate were Carnation milk, to supplement our daily quart of fresh milk, and soda crackers, both of which were bought by the case. Every Saturday, in the days after we gave up keeping chickens of our own, Mamma and Mary would walk to the Farmer's Market to buy a live chicken. In the backyard Mamma would wring its neck and remove the feathers, which she saved to stuff our pillows.

The garden was ready for planting around May 24 when all danger of frost was over and the soil was warm. Mamma would shovel piles of the steaming horse manure that was left along our street into a wheelbarrow, and scoop up mounds of compost from the heap she kept in the backyard and would spread them as fertilizer.

Her backyard garden was a work of art, laid out in carefully tilled plots marked with long pieces of string stretched between two sticks. She would arise at six each summer morning and lovingly nurse her garden, pulling out weeds, plucking insects, hoeing, watering young shoots and tying up the tomato plants — cajoling and caressing to get the very most the garden could yield. By the time we kids awakened, our breakfast — mountains of toast and jam and cups of rich cocoa with Carnation condensed milk — was ready.

The city made free plots of land available within walking distance of our home, for vegetable gardens. I remember Mamma with a few gardening tools, Alfred and Franki reluctantly dragging behind, going to cultivate the plot of land where she usually planted enough potatoes to last us the whole winter. Mamma never grew corn or turnips because they were fed to the pigs in Calabria.

Each season of the year had its own culinary activities. In Spring, with Mary in tow, and a butcher knife in her hand, Mamma would cut the first *cicoria* (dandelion greens) that grew in the ditches and fields close-by, making sure to cut in areas where no dogs had urinated. The greens had to be cut before they flowered so they would not be bitter, and just above the root so the plant would not die. Mamma would boil them and sauté them in garlic and olive oil. Despite Mamma's advice that they were good for the blood, I refused to eat them.

In keeping with the culinary traditions of Calabria, Mamma and Daddy used every growing thing that could be eaten. Late summer and early Fall meant mushroom and berry picking. Sometimes we went on our own; sometimes we joined our relatives. Berry-picking was an all-day adventure to the best blueberry sites that Daddy knew, on the North Branch Road, the Dawson Road or Mount McKay. The whole family piled into the car with baskets of lunch and an assortment of pails and cans. We had fun competing over who could pick the largest and cleanest pail. No matter how bad the black flies, how hot the sun or how much our backs hurt from hours of stooping, we did not complain. When Mamma and Daddy got separated and Mamma shouted, "Luigi, Luigi!" we always giggled. I can recall my shock once when I looked up and saw the tall legs of a man who yelled at me to "get out" because I was trespassing on Indian land. I had never before seen an Indian, and I ran with all my might to tell Daddy, who, about to leave anyway, packed us into the car.

In winter Mamma made a delicious concoction that she called *granita di blueberries*, a sort of sherbet of blueberries, sugar and fresh fallen snow.

I never went mushroom picking, but Alfred and Franki would go with Mamma and Daddy. Daddy was an expert on mushrooms, knew where they grew in abundance and just which ones to pick. The coral coloured *rusitti*, found under the moist woodland covering of fallen twigs and needles, were his first choice, and the *lattari* which emit a milky juice, his second.

I remember their bringing home baskets of them, which would soon fill the kitchen with a fresh woody scent. Mamma would begin cleaning them immediately, spreading the mushrooms on newspapers that covered the kitchen table. Once they were cleaned, she would cook them in boiling water, dropping in a silver twenty-five cent piece which she believed would turn black if the mushrooms were poison. Not once did the coin turn black, and even when I discovered that her test was useless, Mamma continued to use it. Once the mushrooms were cooked, Mamma preserved them in a parsley- and garlic-flavoured brine, in earthenware crocks.

Autumn was the busiest season. Mamma not only harvested the vegetables from the garden, but she carried home baskets of tomatoes, peaches, pears, plums and apricots from Eaton's groceteria downtown. She chopped, squeezed, strained, diced, skinned, cut, peeled, and roasted, to prepare the vegetables and fruit for preserving. The kitchen stove steamed with tubs of boiling water to sterilize the jars that would hold the fruit and vegetables. Nothing was too much work for Mamma. I can't ever remember her going to bed at harvest time.

Before the snow came to stay, our basement cupboards were colourfully stocked with row after row of Mamma's homemade preserves — jars of *conserva* (tomato paste), and of pears, peaches, apricots, plums; strawberry, raspberry, blueberry and grape jam; and orange marmalade; pickled cucumbers and beets; crocks of eggplant, red and green peppers, and of mushrooms.

Daddy built a cold storage room in the basement, where we stored potatoes, cabbage, beets, carrots and squash. The squash harvest was always so plentiful that there weren't enough friends who wanted them, and many just rotted away. Despite this, they were Mamma's pride, since she harvested and planted the seeds from her own special cache. Because the summers were never long enough for the tomatoes to ripen on the vine, we stored the green tomatoes wrapped in newspapers or tissues that Mamma had saved from the Christmas boxes of mandarin oranges. With the addition of several barrels of MacIntosh apples, Mamma and Daddy made certain that there would be more than enough food to feed their five hungry children for the winter.

In late autumn Daddy would cure enough meat from a freshly slaughtered pig to last the winter and well into spring. In Calabria the slaughter of the family pig in January was a joyous social event, with friends and relatives included in the ceremonial ritual. At our place, family as well as relatives and friends were involved in the various stages of preparing the *prisutto*, the *soppressata*, the *capecullo*, and the *sazizze*. The *prisutto* — ham spiced with salt and black pepper — was put on a slatted board in a wooden tub. A heavy rock was then placed on a wooden lid to squeeze out the water.

When all the liquid was drained out, the *prisutto* was hung up to finish curing. The *capecullo* was made of strips of meat from the shoulder and neck, cured with spices, rolled up and then placed in a large casing. The meat for the *soppresata* (salami) and the *sazizze* was ground coarsely and stuffed so tightly into their casings that there were few air spaces that would allow the growth of bacteria.

We kids were allowed to prick the *sazizze* with Mamma's large needles to let the bubbles of air escape, and to help tie up the links with string and hang them to dry on the rafters in the basement. When the *sazizze* were dried sufficiently, they would be coiled in pools of oil in earthenware crocks and stored on the floor of the big basement cupboards. Franki perpetuated Daddy's recipe and methods when he operated his own meat business and passed them on to his son Michael, who now runs the business. "We don't need needles now to prick the air out," Michael explains, "because machines don't let the air in."

Daddy would also make *zuzu* (head cheese) with the left-over meat and pork hocks. He would boil them with bay leaf, red pepper, onion and garlic, then strain the liquid, and recombine it with the meat. The mixture would be put in a cool place in the basement to gel.

Cheese is an important staple in the Calabrese diet, and I recall three varieties that Mamma always had in the pantry: yellow *par-*

miggiano in a huge wedge some of which would be grated by either Franki or Alfred just before we needed it for our pasta dishes; *casucavallo*, an eating cheese, in a thick waxy rind moulded into a pear shape; and the cream-coloured *provolone* that came in balls tied with a long string. We put the *provolone* or *casucavallo* in sandwiches or ate them with fruit.

I remember Daddy making *ricotta*. It would take him hours but it would all be worth the effort. One can scarcely believe that anything could taste so good.

As I grew older, "English" food began appearing on the table. Besides the English Christmas cake, Mamma acquired a taste for English-style white cake. Since she could not bear to throw away the rinds of oranges and lemons, she experimented with them, and soon she was able to use them up making delicious cakes. Mamma also made bushels of deep-fried cake doughnuts (in the "English" fashion), drenched in honey and drizzled with powdered sugar. We must have devoured thousands of these doughnuts when we were young. Mamma's preserves and jams were also made from "English" recipes which the Italian women exchanged among themselves. And Mamma learned to make rice pudding with raisins, milk and a touch of vanilla and nutmeg — creamy and delicious. I never saw her reading recipes. She measured by hand and eye.

Mamma even learned an English verse which she loved to recite before our evening meals:

Thank you for the world so sweet,
Thank you for the food we eat,
Thank you for the birds that sing,
Thank you God for everything.

Although she never attempted making the English pies that I loved, Mamma did attempt once, under duress, to prepare a meal that I insisted must be "English" for an English school-principal I knew. Roast beef and Yorkshire pudding were an Englishman's favourite meal. And so Mamma, who had never cooked such foods in her life served a roast of beef and Yorkshire pudding. I cannot recall what else she prepared. Although our guests were far too polite to reveal any dislike, Mamma's roast was a disaster — leathery, stringy and cooked far too long. And her Yorkshire puddings looked like hockey pucks.

I cannot recall just when I realized that I ate "funny," that our food was different. Nor can I recall when I began to feel ashamed of what I ate. But as an adolescent, I remember feeling embarrassed that we drenched everything in olive oil and garlic; that we ate so much pasta; that we had tall crooked poles to support the beans growing in our garden; that Mamma picked dandelions from the ditches; that she did not make cookies or pies and fancy sandwiches; that we ate flowers of all things — the first yellow flowers from the pumpkins, dipped in egg batter and fried in olive oil.

Why did we have to be so different? Why didn't we sip tea with lemon and munch cookies? Why didn't we have orange juice and cereal for breakfast? Why didn't we have peanut butter and jam sandwiches instead of *provolone* and *frittate*? Why didn't we go out to eat? Why were our platters of cheese and meats not artistically displayed with parsley, watercress or radish roses? When we went on picnics, Mamma used white embroidered linen to spread on the ground, and white cloth napkins, and she wrapped our thick sandwiches in white teacloths. Why didn't we use paper napkins like the "English" and have sandwiches without crusts, neatly packed in wax paper? Why didn't we have corn on the cob and jelly salads all shimmering and moulded?

Once, my next-door Finnish neighbour, Laura, and I took our lunch to Boulevard Lake. She had hot dogs with ketchup. I had *frittate* between thick slices of crusty Italian bread. Her brown bag was pristine dry while mine was soaked with grease.

8
Religion

When the priest slid the grating open in the dark confessional box of St. Andrew's Church, I began to whisper, "Bless me Father for I have sinned. I confess to Almighty God, and to you, Father." St. Andrew's stood at the top of Algoma Street Hill. I felt little and safe beneath its massive columns and arches, its high, slender stained glass windows, its beautifully sculptured wooden pulpit. Watching over me from above were the brightly painted figures of the eight Canadian martyrs: the Jesuit Fathers, Brébeuf, and Lalemant, Chabanel, Daniel, Garnier, Goupil, Jogues and de La Lande. I often meditated on their sufferings at the hands of the Iroquois as I did the Stations of the Cross.

I chose St. Andrew's for confession because the Jesuits in charge did not know me. I sat in the dark pew examining my conscience, trying hard to find sins to confess, and to remember the exact number of times I had told a fib or had "unclean thoughts," whatever that meant.

Sins were categorized as mortal or venial. Mortal sins were grievous and were punished by direct descent into Hell, that terrible place where after death one burned to a crisp for all eternity. Failing to observe the fast on Holy Days of Obligation and missing Mass on Sundays were mortal sins. I recall running up Bay Street hill and down Banning Street to get to Mass before the Gospel started, in order for the Mass to count. Otherwise, I would have to stay for another mass.

Venial sins were minor offenses such as talking back to parents, telling white lies or losing one's temper. They merited Purgatory, the waiting room for Heaven where the soul burned until it was absolutely clean. My little world was filled with fear and dread.

When I felt that I had examined my conscience sufficiently, I chose the box of a confessor who didn't speak too loudly; I would have been mortified if his voice were heard by the other penitents waiting in line. I went behind the deep velvet drapes and knelt in the dark. The grate opened. The priest murmured the words of the prescribed ritual. I recited my confession. Sometimes his manner would scare me into hiding a sin. Then I would plan on confessing it another time and to another confessor. Finally he spoke: "For your penance say three *Our Fathers* and three *Hail Marys*." The grate closed. I had to be on my guard not to sin before receiving Communion the next morning. Nor could I eat, or drink water, after Midnight.

At Mass I couldn't wait to receive the body of Jesus. When the sacred moment came, with eyes downcast and hands clasped, I walked in procession to the altar. The priest put the Host on my tongue. I was afraid to swallow the thin wafer that so mysteriously held the body and blood of Jesus Christ. I was careful not to chew it. If it got stuck on the roof of my mouth, I cautiously licked it off. In absolute union with my God I walked back to my pew. With eyes closed, I sat silently conversing with Him, humbly beseeching Him to help me through my problems. I pledged Him my heart. And it felt good.

Catholics were not supposed to enter a Protestant Church, because in those days the teachings of other faiths were considered heresy. And yet, as a youngster I started going to Sunday School at Bay Street United Church, where the neighbourhood kids went on Sunday afternoons. I liked singing "Jesus Loves Me" and looking at the coloured illustrations of Bible stories. There was no story-telling for kids at the Catholic Church. Besides, the Rev. Mr. Simpson and Mrs. Simpson were so nice to me. Once, they sent us a box of toys with pieces missing here and there. I told Mamma that they came from the Rev. Mr. & Mrs. Simpson. Mrs. Simpson? Could a priest have a wife? Mamma tried to keep me away after that. Surely, the Simpsons would think me ungrateful. After all, they had sent us presents.

It was Mamma's faith and example which inspired and guided me in the Roman Catholic faith. I grew up in an atmosphere of prayer and the strict observance of church discipline.

Daddy left religion to Mamma. Like the typical Southern Italian male he regarded religious observances and churchgoing as *cose femminile* (women's things).

St. Anthony's Church at the corner of Banning and Dufferin was our parish church. It was here that Mamma felt at home when she arrived from Calabria. It was here she heard the familiar Latin and her native tongue.

St. Anthony's has since burned down. But, when I was a child, it was a wondrous place of candles, flowers and incense — and lots of statues. There was Anthony, patron saint of the church, holding the Baby Jesus; Joseph, patron of work and the working man, holding a sheaf of lilies; Barbara, patron of good weather, and Mary, of The Immaculate Conception, with her small bare foot crushing a serpent. In the centre of the high altar was Jesus, with a flaming red heart pierced with thorns exposed on his chest, and his arms wide open, embracing the whole congregation.

Many of the statues were surrounded with lights set in elaborate filigree. There was a marble communion rail and a sanctuary light in the shape of a heart. When the lights went on and the candles flickered, my young eyes were filled with wonder at the beauty of it all. When a bell tinkled, announcing the entrance of the priest, the whole congregation arose to participate in the dramatic re-enactment of the Last Supper — the sacrifice of the Mass. When the priest intoned the "Asperges me" and proceeded up and down the aisles to sprinkle the congregation with holy water, I felt blessed if a drop or two fell on me. St. Anthony's Church was my sanctuary, my shelter against the harshness of school and the tensions at home.

Year after year, the same rituals were important to me. They gave me pleasure and security: the Masses with their beautiful Gregorian chants, the Benediction of the Blessed Sacrament, the Forty Hours' Adoration, the litanies and novenas. I enjoyed reciting the same prayers over and over again: the Latin prayer composed by St. Thomas Aquinas, *Pange lingua gloriosi / Corporis mysterium / Sanguinisque pretiosi* (Sing, my tongue, the Saviour's glory. Of His flesh, the mystery sing); and the prayer composed by St. Ignatius Loyola: "Soul of Christ, sanctify me./ Body of Christ, save me./ Blood of Christ, fill me./ Water from the side of Christ, wash me./ Passion of Christ, strengthen me." I can still hear the priest intoning each line in slowly measured syllables.

In those wonderful days of faith that marked my childhood and adolescence, I loved the Lenten and Christmas rituals best. On Ash Wednesday, the priest dabbed ashes on our foreheads with the reminder, "Ashes you are and to ashes you will return." On Holy Thursday, the Ladies of the Altar Society took great pride in beautifying the Altar of Repose. I recall my eyes feasting on the altar resplendent with Easter lilies and candlelight. Mamma used to go late in the night to keep Our Lord company in his final hours.

The next day, Good Friday, was the saddest day of the year for me. At church, no candles were lit; no organ was played; no bells were rung or holy communion given. At home Mamma would not allow us to play. It was a day of mourning. At three o'clock in the afternoon I would make the Stations of the Cross and meditate on Christ's selfless love for us, even unto death. Oh how sorry I felt for my sins which had helped crucify my Lord. My ingratitude shamed me. I pleaded, "Jesus, my Lord, my God, my all, how can I love Thee as I ought?"

Many years later on a blistering hot day in Jerusalem I recited the same plea and made the Stations of the Cross with four hundred students from the Sorbonne in Paris, walking from Pilate's Palace to the crucifixion site at Calvary. The students were barefoot and three of them carried heavy wooden crosses. As we slowly edged our way along the narrow Via Dolorosa, in the very footsteps Our Lord had trod nearly two thousand years ago, I marvelled at the piety of the young pilgrims. As for my own devotion, I found my attention straying to the painted red toenails of the girls.

I remember getting up very very early on Holy Saturday to attend the solemn ceremonies which fascinated me: the blessing of the new fire, the paschal candles and the holy water. My Chicago cousin, Rose Elia, remembers that when the bells tolled the end of Lent, her mother lay on the floor, her arms stretched out to thrash away the evil spirits, and recited, "*Uscite serpente della casa mia, che e risurcitato il Signore mio*" (Depart evil spirits from my house because my Saviour is risen).

The rock rolled away from the tomb and the triumph over death is a mystery that the years would interpret, but a new-born Holy Babe was cause for immediate joy. It meant feasts and carols, joyful family gatherings and special religious services. When, as children, we were allowed to go to Midnight Mass on Christmas Eve, we felt we were the luckiest kids in the world. Mamma made sure that we arrived early because it was one time of the year our little church was packed to the doors.

The church at Christmas was a festival of flaming poinsettias and dazzling light. The enormous elevated *Presepio* (manger scene) with its figures of the Holy Family, the shepherds, the Magi and the barnyard animals was built at one end of the altar and surrounded by evergreen trees. The fragrance of pine and the sweet pungency of incense floated through the air. From the choir loft, the trumpets of the organ burst into jubilant peals. And the angelic voices of my cousins, Agatha and Carmen Sisco, and Frank Covello, sang to greet the new born child: "Angels we have heard on high," "O Holy Night," "Adeste Fedelis." And we waited in quiet reverence for the magic of the midnight hour.

Mamma was piously raised in the Roman Catholic faith, but medieval superstitions with which she had grown up in Calabria, lingered. Much as she sought to repress them, she feared them. The *mal'occhio* (the "evil eye"), for instance, was attracted to beauty, excellence, strength and wealth. Its dread gaze had the power to inflict all sorts of misfortune. And she feared the *affascino*, the spell which an envious person casts upon his or her victim. She showed me how to make the traditional defense against the evil eye by pointing the sign of the horn made with the thumb tucked under the second and third fingers, with the first and fourth fingers extended, and saying, *"Fore mal'occhio"* (Go away, evil eye). Although her habitual expressions to undo the possible malevolence were pious phrases such as *"Benedica"* (God bless) or *"Madonna mia, aiutame"* (Mother of God, help me) or *"Madonna mia, duname forza"* (Mother of God, give me strength), I have heard her say, on occasion, *"Non ci capisi lu mal'occhio"* (May the evil eye not strike).

Mamma was wont to rejoice at other people's successes and say *"Chi Dio ti benedica"* (God bless you) or *"Beato u latte che t'ha dato mammata"* (Blessed be the milk that your mother gave you), or *"Beato le minne chi ti hanno allatato"* (Blessed be the breasts that suckled you).

Mamma's belief in the protective power of the saints was strong: St. Anthony recovered lost articles; Christopher protected travellers; Roch healed sores. On February 3, each year Mamma took us to church to have our throats blessed with two crossed candles and to ask for the intercession of St. Blaise who had saved a child from choking to death on a fishbone. On December 13, she honoured Lucy, patron saint of eyesight. There was reason for this. I was short-sighted, had worn glasses since Grade VIII when the school nurse informed me I had myopia. I had complained to Mamma that this was caused by a defect in the eye's construction, that it was hereditary, and could not be cured. She decided to get supernatural help and invoked St. Lucy's aid. One year, she made a novena to her, culminating in visits to the homes of a few friends to solicit funds for a High Mass to be sung in Lucy's honour. So sincere was she that, in keeping with Catholic tradition, she humbled herself by going barefoot into the homes. According to legend Lucy is honoured among virgin martyrs because she plucked out her beautiful eyes in order to preserve her virginity and her eyesight was miraculously restored. In art she is depicted holding two eyeballs on a tray.

As added protection, Mamma wore the brown scapular of Our Lady of Mount Carmel and a number of miraculous medals in a little pouch attached to her brassiere with a safety pin. Often she would forget to unfasten the pouch before her undergarment was washed, so the scapular and medals went into the washing machine.

Mamma was especially devoted to Our Lady, the Blessed Virgin Mary, honoured by Roman Catholics worldwide as the Seat of Wisdom, Gate of Heaven, and Refuge of Sinners, and the most powerful of saints in interceding with God who refuses nothing to His mother.

Each year on July 16, Our Lady of Mount Carmel's feast day, Mamma took several hours, no matter how busy she was, to spend with Our Lady in private adoration. The Sisco family had special devotion to Our Lady of Mount Carmel, because as an eight-year-old, Mamma's brother, Giovanni, who had been told not to go near the water, disobeyed and was caught in a whirlpool. He called on Our Lady of Mount Carmel and miraculously found himself on shore. From the time she was a young lady, Mamma never failed to honour the debt the Sisco family owed to Our Lady of Mount Carmel.

The salvation of her immortal soul was Mamma's spiritual goal in life. She made novenas to Our Lady of Pompeii, and, from the age of nineteen, she devoted an hour, between two and three in the afternoon on the 23rd of each month, to the recitation of the Rosary, to gain the grace of a happy death.

Each year, on December 4, Mamma would be "at home" to her friends who would gather to celebrate the feast day of St. Barbara, the patron saint of her town. Oh, how busy she would be on that day, making *panetelli*, little loaves of St. Barbara's bread, and other baked delicacies. She would set the table with a white tablecloth and napkins, trays of sliced cheeses, father's home-made meats, bowls of green olives and of dried black olives that had been soaked in oil and oregano. At the end of the meal she would serve her own homemade brandied cherries which she kept stored in jars for years at a time. When I came home from school, the aroma of coffee filled the air. Mamma was happy. All was well in the world.

After her guests left, she would place the *panetelli* on the ledges of the windows to protect our home from thunder and lightning, reciting as she went several ritual verses of an epic poem honouring St. Barbara. She taught us kids, this simple stanza:

Santa Barbara
Fa bon tiempu
Ca mo passanu dui galeri
una de acqua e una da viento
Santa Barbara
Fa bon tiempu

(Saint Barbara
Make good weather
Because two evils are raging
One of water and one of wind
Saint Barbara
Make good weather).

December 4 was also the day when my Uncle John, Mamma's brother, treated every student at St. Joseph's School to an apple. Since his grocery store was just across the street, we walked the short distance, lined up in double file to receive our apples. Year after year he continued this practice, honouring the patron saint of his hometown.

Long before Father Peyton campaigned over the air with the slogan *The family that prays together stays together*, Mamma had practised what he preached. Every night for years, just before bedtime, Mamma gathered her five children in front of the kitchen stove. Sitting in a rocking chair with her brood kneeling about her, she would lead us through the Rosary. On Mondays and Thursdays we meditated on the Joyful Mysteries; Tuesdays and Fridays, on the Sorrowful; and Saturdays and Sundays on the Glorious. An assortment of prayers followed, usually concluding with the Litany of Saints, the longest of all the Litanies, while her children, heavy with sleep, would respond automatically with the Latin refrain *Ora pro nobis, ora pro nobis* (Pray for us, pray for us). As if that weren't enough, she would add indulgenced ejaculations beseeching the angels and a battery of saints in heaven: Santa Liberata, Santo Francesco di Paolo among others. Finally Mamma made the sign of the cross and lifted the cross of the Rosary to her lips. We could go to bed.

For years, we prayed for a brick house. Mamma's heart was set on one. Her house in Piane Crati had been a solid stone *palazzo* made to last for centuries. Even though Daddy covered our frame house with stucco, and I delighted in the sparkles the pieces of coloured glass gave off when the sun hit them, Mamma considered it inferior to her stone *palazzo*. Years later, while I was teaching in Chapleau, Mamma wrote to tell me that they had moved into a brick home, as high as her *palazzo*.

Remembering and respecting the dead is a sacred Italian *dovere* (duty). Each year on All Souls Day, Mamma faithfully registered the names of her closest relatives to be remembered at Mass in order to hasten their passage to Heaven. Anytime she mentioned their names she immediately added the words *buon anima* (good soul). When they visited her in her dreams as they often did, she would try to interpret what they had said. She did things in the name of the dead and believed that the souls in Purgatory could obtain blessings for their friends on earth.

Mamma also performed good works to prepare herself for the "other world." She hand-stitched delicate gold threads in altar cloths. She made vestments for the priests and coffin drapes. She gave to the poor and to her favourite charities in Italy. Even during the hard times of the Depression, she made sacrifices in our house to send money to them. Whenever I used the words "diplomas" or "certificates" she was quick to remind me that she herself had two diplomas, two credentials attesting to her good works, which I later found while I was cleaning out her trunks: *A Diploma de Benefice*, dated June 16, 1954, that entitled her to masses in perpetuity at the Basilica of St. Anthony of Padua, and *a Diploma di Benemerenza* from *l'orfanotrofio Antoniano Femminile di Taormina*, dated May 26, 1967, that assured her, as a faithful benefactress of the Orphanage, of special plenary indulgences.

When I left home Mamma gave me a sacred talisman — a picture of the Sacred Heart of Jesus. On the back she wrote:

> Cuore di Gesu alle vostri mani io raccommando la mia figlia Serafina. Voi me la proteggete. Voi me la guidate. Voi me la serbate da ogni pericolo.
>
> (Heart of Jesus in your hands I commend my daughter Serafina. You will protect her. You will guide her. You will save her from every danger.)

The picture is now tattered and dog-eared, but I still carry it in my wallet. The Sacred Heart of Jesus is real to me. Through the years I have made deals with the Sacred Heart, said novenas, lit candles, offered Masses, and sent monies to charity in His honour.

I still have the holy prayer cards sent to me from my Grandmother Serafina who, it was said, when she was leaving the church, never turned her back to the altar. I collected them as devoutly as my brothers collected their hockey cards.

I can remember how honoured I felt, when, at the age of fourteen, Monsignor Tomaselli asked me to be the organist at St. Anthony's. I didn't even ask him if I was going to be paid. But at the end of the first month, his assistant, Father Daley, gave me a cheque for one dollar. As I was sitting on the organ bench, he put his hand on my right wrist, and instructed me "to save it for a rainy day."

When Father Truffa arrived in 1940, he replaced the old pump organ with an electric one-keyboard Hammond. Oh how I loved to play it! With a musical genius as the pastor, the choir sang the beautiful Masses written for voices with organ accompaniment, such as the "Mass in honour of the Immaculate Conception of the Blessed Virgin Mary," by John Wiegand. Many were the happy hours I spent at home practising my church music. But of all the music that lingers in my memory, Father Truffa's arrangements for *Panis Angelicus* and *Ave Verum* are the dearest.

There was a time in my late teens when I contemplated becoming a nun. I recall telling this to my music teacher, Sister V. Being a practical woman, she advised me not to tell Mother Superior that I knew how to do anything.

"What do you mean?" I asked.

"Well, if you say that you can sew and cook and teach, you'll be doing all those jobs," she explained. I did not enter the convent.

My childhood church had its rigours and its duties, but it has given me the sureness and comfort that come with belief. It gave me my prayers in English. The words of *The Magnificat*, Mary's song of exultation — those beautiful words from Luke I — still lift my spirits heavenwards: "My soul doth magnify the Lord: And my spirit hath rejoiced in God my Saviour. Because He hath regarded the humility of His Handmaid: for, behold, from henceforth all generations shall call me blessed." Words as glorious as any written by Shakespeare.

9
School Days: Cornwall and St. Joseph's

I was four and a half when I was enrolled at Cornwall School, only a stone's throw from our house. To get me in, Mamma's friend, who registered me, said that I was six. I was terrified. I could not speak one word of English.

One day soon after registration we were asked to bring a cup and saucer from home for a school party. That afternoon our teacher held them up and asked us to identify our own. I was so timid that I was simply unable to raise my hand to acknowledge mine. I remained frozen at my desk.

Later that year on a cold winter's morning I arrived a few minutes late and could not open the heavy doors of the school. I didn't know what to do. I went back home, so afraid to tell Mamma that I just stood in our backyard. If it had not been for the breadman who told her there was a little girl shivering outside, I might have died from hypothermia.

In the second grade, we began writing with straight pens. For weeks, one of the braids of the little blonde girl sitting in front of me kept swinging across my inkwell. The day came when I could resist no longer. I dipped the tip of her braid in the ink. The teacher gave me such a beating with a heavy black leather strap that my left wrist swelled and burned for a week. But I never showed Mamma the welts. Mamma had great respect for teachers and believed they were always right. Didn't she come from Calabria where a teacher was addressed with the same title of respect *Don/Donna* as was given other professionals such as doctors and lawyers?

Flavio F. tells a more chilling story. His teacher summoned Eileen B's father to the school. When the teacher told him about his daughter's misdemeanours, he beat her up in front of the Grade VII class. The teacher was always right.

By the time I was six, somehow, as if by magic, I had learned to read. I could read the entire Red Primer. And a wonderful new world opened up to me. It was inhabited by animals that talked and did such ridiculous things: a little pig who went to market, a little red hen who made bread and a donkey who put its feet on a window sill. Wind, rain, and dandelions talked too. It was a child's world peopled by the mischievous Goldilocks, by Henny Penny, and by a gingerbread boy who ran away from home and was eaten up. I was fascinated with poetry, the joy of rhyme, rhythm, repetition and merriment. I loved to read aloud. I chanted over and over:

> *If you try and try and try,*
> *And do not pout or cry,*
> *You will find by and by,*
> *It is best to try and try.*

I could not hold a tune, but I loved my Music class. Miss Miskimmins taught us *Home Sweet Home*, the signature song of the famous prima donna Adeline Patti: "Mid pleasures and palaces though we may roam/ Be it ever so humble there's no place like home." I still love the words.

Mamma and Daddy never read to us. We had no stories at bedtime. Nor could they help me with my reading. My Primer was the only English book in our home. (Except for Daddy's explosives manual, my parents never owned any English books.) But I read my Primer over and over to myself, to Mamma, to my younger brothers and sisters, to anyone who would listen. I knew every page by heart.

The First Book, too, presented a fantastic world: a prince who was transformed into a frog, kittens who lost their mittens, and a tortoise who raced with a hare. I read them again and again. Some of the pieces were taken from literary masters such as Robert Louis Stevenson, Alfred Lord Tennyson, and Charles Kingsley. The short verses that filled the spaces between stories of the *First Book* were full of intriguing rhymes:

> *Little drops of water*
> *Little grains of sand*
> *Make the mighty ocean*
> *And the pleasant land.*

The Second Book lured me to new places and people through stories, such as "How the Greeks took Troy," and "Queen Bess and Walter Raleigh." I lived under the spell of "Wynken, Blynken and Nod." By the time I was eight, I had become hooked on a world of words — English words. I always won the Spelling Bees.

After four years at Cornwall Public School, Mamma sent me to St. Joseph's, a Catholic school; she must have been threatened with excommunication. St. Joseph's was two blocks further away than Cornwall, at the corner of John and Ontario Streets.

Going there had its dangers. On the way we were taunted by the Cornwall School boys who would shout, "Catholics, Catholics go to Hell/ Protestants, Protestants ring the bell." The St. Joseph boys would shout back, "Salvation Army, save my Soul/ Send it to Heaven in a sugar bowl." And then the fights would begin. Big boys washed my face with snow. They stung my heart with "Dago" and "Wop." When I was out of their reach I screamed back the counter-spell: "Sticks and stones will break my bones/ But names will never hurt me." Once, a serious fight erupted. A Cornwall kid stabbed my brother Franki with a knife in the back of the neck. Outraged, Alfred lashed out with his fists and scattered the Cornwall kids in all directions.

St. Joseph's operated in regimented routine. We lined up outside, in double file — boys at the boys' door, girls at the girls' door. Not until our lines were absolutely straight were we ordered to march forward. Then we marched to the martial music played by a senior student at the piano, and to the "Left! Right!" which the nun on outdoor duty beat out with her yardstick. My friend Verna recalls that one time, when she was in line, a commotion broke out. One girl had a black and white prayer card bearing the likeness of St. Theresa of the Little Flower. She claimed that if Verna stared at five marked spots for thirty seconds then looked up at the sky Verna would miraculously see the saint's image. Verna laughed at her. This created such a fuss that the nun on duty took Verna out of line and strapped her.

As soon as we entered our classrooms, we stood by our desks which were screwed to the floor. The snap of a rubber band against a prayer book or a tap on the desk bell signified an order to kneel, get up, sit down, stand, turn right or left, or go forward. When we were dismissed for lunch and at four o'clock, we knelt on the floor to pray. When we answered a question we stood at attention, and when we were not writing, we sat looking straight ahead with our hands behind our back. We were trained marionettes.

We prayed a lot — before classes started and after they finished; in the morning, at noon and at four o'clock. I went along with the classroom chorus — the Apostle's Creed, the Confiteor, and the Lord's Prayer murmuring, "Lead us not into Penn Station." I didn't see the words in print until years later. I remember we were always praying for the conversion of Russia. I loved to recite "The Angelus" best, especially the lines, "Behold the handmaid of the Lord/ May it be done unto me according to Thy word." The one picture in the whole school that I still remember is a reproduction of Millet's *The Angelus*, showing two peasants stopping their work in the field to pray.

Catechism was taught as a drill. Question: Who made you? Answer: God made me. Question: Who is God? etc. We were also drilled on the Ten Commandments. Attendance at Sunday Mass was checked rigorously. During Lent a large grid with the names of every student was displayed on the blackboard. Gold stars would be placed next to a student's name to indicate attendance at Mass. Those who went every day got picture prayer cards as prizes.

Composition was a once-a-year event. From Grades VI to VIII, I was assigned the same topic every year: "How I spent my summer holidays." By the time I reached Grade VIII, I was bored with the topic, so that year I copied a story about finding a hornet's nest, from a magazine. I didn't even know what a hornet was. For weeks I worried that my teacher would find out what I had done. But our compositions were never returned.

Science was overlooked entirely. Our one quasi-scientific project, repeated every autumn, was to collect weeds, dry them and identify them. I recall keeping mine pressed between newspapers for months under my bed because the teacher never required us to submit them.

Teachers were the undisputed figures of authority in the classroom; their word was law. It was a common sight to see the teacher with a ruler or yardstick in hand, as she patrolled the aisles, whacking the knuckles of students who were whispering, making noise or chewing gum. Discipline could range from corporal punishment to writing out *Procrastination is the thief of time* five hundred times on foolscap. Rita N. remembers that Sister F., the principal, whom we called The Battle-Axe, hit Edwin M's face so hard against the blackboard that his nose bled. Several times my Grade VIII teacher gave me the strap because, in my eagerness, I blurted out the answer before she called on me. At other times, she would confine me to the cloakroom. If, while I was in there, I heard the principal coming with the large beads on her rosary clicking, I used to hide among the coats which hung on hooks. One time the teacher forgot to give me permission to leave for lunch and I spent the whole noon hour in the cloakroom. I went hungry that day.

But the teachers did not have a monopoly on violence. When I was nine years old I had to sit across from the class bully. He was one of the "dummies," eight years older than I. Suddenly, one day he struck a compass through my new Highroad's Dictionary and jabbed a hole right through it. I cherished my books.

And my first Dictionary was dear to me. But I held back my tears. I knew enough not to tell the teacher, and she never found out. I used my damaged dictionary for years afterwards.

On rare occasions students retaliated. When Sister F. tried to give J.J. the strap, he bit her hand. I remember vividly the day, in 1934, when Frank K. was punished in front of the class. Sister R. had given him one lash, when, all of a sudden, Frank socked her in the jaw. The class gasped in one voice. We never saw Frank again.

I thrived at school. I was Miss Goody-Two-Shoes. Once when my Grade VIII teacher dictated a sight passage about Pope Pius XI, I was the only student who, in writing it out, spelled the Pope's name correctly. I could memorize anything with ease — the multiplication tables and all the rules of grammar, for instance. I became such a proficient "grammarian" that I was able to parse words and analyze sentences from difficult prose passages, and poems such as Milton's *Paradise Lost*. I memorized all the information the teacher wanted us to know about the countries of the world. When she placed her long wooden pointer on a river, city, mountain range, or lake on the wall map, I shouted out the name, without waiting to be chosen. That's when I would be sent to the cloakroom or get the strap. I loved maps and would spend hours at home tracing them on tissue paper, placing the original and the tissue against the windows to see the outlines better.

I made relief maps from a mixture of flour, salt and water on cardboard. After these dried, I coloured the lakes and rivers blue, and the land green. I had so much fun. It was easy because borders and names remained constant in those days. I remember memorizing the counties of Southern Ontario as well as their capitals. But when I asked the teacher what county Port Arthur was in, she told me sternly that Port Arthur was in a "district" and left it at that. Her disapproving eyes told me not to pursue the subject. The teacher was never wrong. My sister, Rita, recalls telling her Grade III teacher that she had seen no trees in Sudbury. The teacher told her that she was lying. All we had to do was regurgitate what the teacher said. And I did.

Ontario education was British in substance. British and Canadian were synonymous. I memorized the British money system and the British liquid and linear measures. I memorized the achievements of the British around the world: the signing of the Magna Charta, the invention of the steam engine, the defeat of the Boers. I applauded Robert Clive avenging the Black Hole of Calcutta, Wolfe at the Plains of Abraham, Wellington at Waterloo, General Gordon at Khartoum. My heroes were British: Francis Drake, the dashing buccaneer, Florence Nightingale, the Lady with the Lamp, and Horatio Nelson whose last words at the battle of Trafalgar were "Thank God, I have done my duty."

Our studies never included Italian explorers, inventors, scientists or artists. Nobody we studied had names like Pasquale or Celestino, let alone Peppina and Nunziata. At the age of ten when I had to choose a confirmation name, I selected the most English of all names — Elizabeth — after the popular young princess and an English Queen. It was Mamma who told me about the great Galileo, and about Michelangelo who struck his hammer on Moses' knee because it was so life-like and asked him, "*E perché non parli?*" (Why don't you speak?). It was Mamma who spoke proudly of Calabria, raising her right leg and pointing to her toe to show me that her province was located at the toe of Italy's boot. It was Mamma who told me that it was a *Calabrisella* (a girl from Calabria) who had won "the beauty contest," as she put it, adding no further details. But Mamma's opinion did not count. She was not part of my school life. She did not knit shawls for the nuns. She did not make chocolate fudge for the school's candy sales. She never once visited the school or talked to a teacher on the telephone.

My history classes did mention Columbus and Cabot. Our textbook, *Junior History of England*, read, "The American discoveries of Columbus and Cabot awakened the old seafaring spirit of the English people, and during the Tudor period many distinguished sailors found their way into strange seas." The text went on to enumerate the English achievements. There is no mention that Columbus and Cabot were Italians. But it wasn't Columbus or Cabot, Michelangelo or Galileo who caught my imagination. It was the picture of the English explorer, Henry Hudson, and his little son cast adrift by his mutinous crew in a small boat on James Bay.

According to the *Ontario Dept. of Education Courses of Study for the Public and Separate Schools* (June, 1934), "The teacher should not fail to emphasize the extent, power, and responsibilities of the British Empire, its contributions to the highest form of civilization, the achievements of its statesmen and its generals, and the increasingly important place that Canada holds amongst the Overseas Dominion."

My love of English words grew as did the power of the British Empire. I memorized with delight those magnificent poems proclaiming England's might: "England, my England," "Ye Mariners of England" and "Rule Brittania." I was proud to be part of the greatest empire the world had ever known. I knew more about Wordsworth's "Daffodils" than about Duncan Campbell Scott's "Night Hymns on Lake Nipigon." I knew more about the Druids and Stonehenge than about the Ojibway who lived on the reserve at Mount McKay in Fort William. Each time I looked at the map of the world and saw all the countries coloured pink from west to east, I said to myself, "Yes, it is true that the sun never sets on the British Empire.

Yes, to be British is best. Brittania, rule the waves."

10
Port Arthur Collegiate Institute

When I registered at the Port Arthur Collegiate Institute, the principal, Mr. Sinclair, wrote down my name as Sarah Fina. "But Serafina is my first name," I explained.

He had never heard the name before. "How do you spell it?" he asked.

"*S-e-r-a-f-i-n-a*. My surname is Petrone."

"How do you spell that?" he asked.

"*P-e-t-r-o-n-e.*"

"Petron," he pronounced it.

"No, Petronè," I corrected him. Very few Italians attended PACI, so Mr. Sinclair's ignorance of Italian names was not surprising.

Out of perhaps ninety students who enrolled when I did (the total student body was four hundred) there may have been only three other students of Italian descent. And in four years' time they had dropped out. During my entire life at PACI I was the only person in the school whose name was Serafina. I didn't need a last name, never even put my surname on any test or examination paper. But I hated my name.

It did not take me long to discover just what a closed, predominantly WASP enclave, Port Arthur Collegiate was. I lived in the South End — the wrong end of the city. South-enders did not go to the Collegiate but to the Port Arthur Technical and Commercial High School. My brothers, Alfred and Franki, went to the "Tech." So did my neighbourhood girlfriends, Helvi H., Helvi L. and Laura A. I had no choice if I wanted an academic diploma, as I very much did. The Collegiate was the only place to get one.

I knew my years there were going to be unpleasant, but I had not fully anticipated what an ordeal they would turn out to be. To begin with, there was a terrible cliquishness in the school. The students lived in the "right" sections of town: Mariday Park, St. Patrick's Square, Prospect, Peter, and College Streets. They spent summers together at their cottages on Loon Lake and along the beaches of Lake Superior. They got elected to every school office. Their parents belonged to the same fashionable clubs and went to the same Protestant churches. The mothers belonged to the same church groups. The fathers were members of the City Council, the Board of Education and the Rotary Club. My father was a labour gang foreman. And my mother spoke broken English. They did not belong to the right social clubs.

I envied my female classmates. I envied their self-assurance, their sophistication, their spending money, their flare for clothes, their comely looks, and even their freckled noses. They seemed witty, easy and casual around boys. I wanted to go with them to *Rudils* after school for a cherry coke or a malted milk. On

Friday afternoons I wanted to go with them to watch the inter-school rugby games. And to sing with the crowd:

Beer Beer for PACI
Shake up the cocktails
Pour on the rye
Send somebody out for gin
And don't let a sober person in
We never stumble
We never fall
We sober up on wood alcohol.

I even harboured a secret wish to be a cheerleader in my cute, red-and-white pleated skirt. I wanted to be one of the girls waving her red and white pom-poms and turning cartwheels.

But the cheerleaders were stuck-up. They were the "mucky-mucks" with their blue eyes, blonde hair and fair skin. I was an awkward and skinny twelve year old. I wore glasses. I hated them. I hated being called "four eyes." And my olive complexion was covered with acne. No matter what I tried — staying away from oily and greasy foods or putting on calamine lotion — I could not get rid of the pesky pimples. In the summer I baked for hours under the hot sun trying to burn them out. I consoled myself with Mamma's constant reminder: *Chi bella vo parire/Gran dolore addi sofrire*. Succinctly put, "No pain, no gain." But in the winter the acne reappeared in full force. Despite Mamma's protests I just could not stop my nervous habit of squeezing the pimples. That made them even worse.

In Grade X, my first year at PACI (I had gone to St. Joseph's Academy for my Grade IX) the class rep invited me to play a piano solo at a class party. I had never been to a school party. I had never been to a school dance. I really didn't know what was called for. I chose one of my impressive pieces, Chopin's *Polonaise in A*. The applause was polite. I had been rejected. That was my last school party. My yearning to be accepted by my classmates remained in my private thoughts unexpressed.

Another incident, during my last year at PACI, has riveted itself in memory. A classmate, Helene C., with whom I had established a good rapport through our musical studies at St. Joseph's Convent, invited me to a Christmas party which she was giving at the exclusive Shuniah Club on the top floor of the Whalen Building. It was the first time I had been invited to a real party. Initially, I was elated to have been asked, but elation soon shifted to uncertainty. I could not possibly go alone. Helene agreed that I could bring my Croation friend, Theresa.

Mamma and I went shopping for a dress. In those days, there was no "teen-age" market. We all wore grown-up clothes. It was wartime, of course, and there was not much choice. We selected an expensive olive-green princess-style dress with thirty-six matching covered buttons on the back.

When I entered the huge ballroom, I was intimidated. I knew instantly I was out of place. Because I had heard that hats were *de rigueur* for afternoon events, I had kept on my rust-coloured felt hat with its large brim and long peacock feather tilted provocatively over my right eye. I was the only girl wearing a hat, and I was too self-conscious to return to the dressing room to take it off. Instead, I walked to a chair against the wall, my knees shaking and my heart pounding. I sat down and could not move, not even to help myself to the buffet table. I ate nothing. No one except Helene, her brother and parents came to talk to Theresa and me. Everyone was making merry. The band played fun pieces, such as "Three Little Fishies," "Mairzy Doates," "My Mamma Done Tole Me," and "Flat Foot Floogy with the Floy Floy." In silence, I watched my classmates swing and jitterbug and boogie-woogie. Perhaps, I thought, if I were asked to dance once, the boys would see how well I danced and would ask me again. (Because of Daddy's teaching, I was a good dancer). Then Helene's brother did ask me. But I was so nervous and awkward that I kept stepping on his shoes — it was a disaster. And dancing with my hat on probably made me look ludicrous. I wanted to be invisible. Theresa and I were the first to leave.

"Perhaps, if I had not worn my hat," I queried Theresa.

She replied calmly, "I doubt whether that would have made any difference."

No more was said. When I arrived home, I did not tell Mamma how we had been treated.

The events of World War II, which started when I was in Grade XII, made things worse for me. I was Italian — "Eyetalian" as my classmates pronounced it. Not only was I on the wrong side of town I was on the wrong side of the war. I was called *wop* and *dago* to my face. "Enemy alien" was another label. Belittling jokes — such as "Did you stomp on the grapes with your bare feet last night?" or "Is it true that Eyetalians eat pigeons and sparrows?" — reflected the terrible underlying prejudice that prevailed. I accepted the ridicule and never fought back, concealing my embarrassment and shame. But I hated my *differentness*.

Having no close friend, I walked alone to and from the Collegiate, too shy to pass directly by the soldiers who congregated around the Armouries at the corner of Secord and Park Streets. At home my parents were blissfully unaware of my inner turmoil.

With no social or other school life to distract me from learning, I immersed myself into my studies. In team sports I was the proverbial "last picked." However, I was a very fast runner and good in Calisthenics. I excelled in Latin, French, History and English Literature. A few classmates copied my homework and even my examination answers. I was too much of a coward to say "No." Secretly I wished that the teachers would catch them, but they never did.

All the teachers had "English" surnames. Whether they shared the students' discrimination against Italians, I am not sure. I showed my teachers deference. I handed in excellent work.

Only on two occasions did teachers take notice of my crippling shyness. In exasperation, my Grade X English teacher reprimanded me in class. "Shy people are self-centred," she said flatly. I crept lower in my seat, ashamed and resentful and silent. Three years later, My Grade XIII English teacher asked me to meet her after class. That day we had read our favourite ballad. I had chosen "Kirconnell Lea." I had begun, "I wish I were where Helen lies/Night and day on me she cries." And then I got so nervous I could barely finish the poem. In private she assured me that my work was very good. I had no need to have an inferiority complex. "But I am Italian," I said. I never forgot her reply: "You should consider yourself lucky. You have two cultures to draw upon." It has taken me decades to appreciate the wisdom of her reply.

Because I had not studied Algebra at St. Joseph's Academy, the senior maths teacher agreed to teach me for fifteen minutes two mornings a week, before the first class. At the end of the year, not knowing exactly how to show my gratitude, I gingerly gave her a box of chocolates from Mamma's trunk. I didn't know whether this was an appropriate gesture until many years later when this teacher and I belonged to the same professional group, and she told me how impressed she had been. Even then, I was not eager to pursue the topic, because I recalled my girlfriend's accusation that Petrone chocolates always smelled of mothballs.

During the four years I spent at PACI I found consolation in scores of literary passages that threw light on my world. Shylock's speech was especially relevant: "Hath not a Jew eyes? Hath not a Jew hands, organs, dimensions, senses, affections, passions?... If you prick us do we not bleed? If you tickle us, do we not laugh? If you poison us, do we not die?"

I tried hard to erase the *Italianness* that the dominant culture despised. I tried to determine just what made me so foreign. Was it my name? my appearance? my skin colour? my breath? my body smell, my food? the language I spoke? I could not change my colour. I refused to eat food with garlic and strong flavours. I was very conscious of BO and bad breath. I had a very good command of the English language. And I spoke it without an Italian accent. In my assimilationist hurry, I cringed with embarrassment whenever Mamma screamed at the top of her voice or gesticulated with her hands or removed the chamber pot from under her bed. I was certain that "English" people did none of those things.

I decided to change my baptismal name. No matter how it was pronounced or spelled,

I bore a despised Italian name in an English-speaking country. When I had started at Cornwall, the name was spelled *Serafiina*. Since I lived in a Finnish area, the teachers had put in a double *i* as in Finnish words. The teachers at St. Joseph's School had a variety of spellings: *Sarafina, Serafrina, Serafine, Serabine* and *Sarfina*. On my birth certificate it was spelled *Sarafine*. My Roman Catholic music teachers spelled it *Seraphine* or *Seraphina*, the Italian feminine diminutive of the Hebrew *seraphim*, one of the six winged angels of the highest rank. I don't know why I spelled it *Serafina* — perhaps because my paternal grandmother spelled it that way. No matter how it was spelled or pronounced, my Italian name in all its variations was anathema to me. I winced when I heard it called or saw it written. For years I kept up a search for another Serafina, but it was futile until in the 1960s, I read Tennessee Williams' play *The Rose Tattoo*, and found a "Serafina," the heroine of the play. I was elated. I read the play three times in quick succession. But I still have not met another living *Serafina*.

What's more, the pronunciation and spelling of my surname varied — from *Betroni* as it was written in the Register when I started school, to such variants as *Petron, Petroni, Petrona* and *Patrone*. Although I was determined to change my first name, I could not change my surname. When I was advised to anglicize it, years later, at the Ontario College of Education, because of the Wasp nature of the high school establishment, I refused. Ontario in those days was an Orange-dominated, bigoted province where Jews and Italians were openly discriminated against.

What's in a name? "'Tis but thy name that is my enemy," Juliet tells Romeo.

At seventeen I re-named myself *Penny*. My Croation friend Lola selected my new monicker. She was constantly saying to me, "A penny for your thoughts." That was it. I was Penny Petrone. The alliteration appealed to my English sense of sound.

Mamma steadfastly refused to call me *Penny*. And I was still *Serafina* at PACI. But in the larger world, I gradually became known as *Penny Petrone*.

Finally, I graduated, leaving the WASP stronghold forever.

Mamma knew that I was smart and wondered whether she should send me to university. She needed assurance that she would be doing the right thing. She went to the pastor at St. Anthony's and to an "English" friend of Daddy's for advice. Both counselled her against it. Mamma was raised in the peasant world of Calabria where there was no mobility. She belonged to a people with no expectations; their outlook placing self-imposed limits on ambition. *"Chine si contenta guorra"* (Whoever is contented rejoices), she would often say. And her religious upbringing had stressed the passive acceptance of one's station in life. She was not going to push her luck.

Only *gli Inglesi* were expected to go to university. In 1941, the year I graduated from PACI, Port Arthur's population was 24,426. Of this number, 13,045 were of Anglo-Saxon origin and 1,132 of Italian. I was the only graduate of Italian parentage in both my Junior Matriculation and Senior Matriculation years. I went to Teachers' College — "Normal School," as it was called in those days.

11
War Years

The war catapulted the nation out of the economic despair of the Depression into a booming war-time economy which meant that suddenly there were plenty of jobs. The flow of drifters who came to our house begging for food, ended abruptly, and for the first time in his life, Daddy was able to find a year-round job. Mamma's prayers had been answered.

A new era of prosperity hit the Head of the Lakes. Industries which had been shut down for over a decade were re-opened. The Canada Car plant in Fort William began producing aircraft. By the end of the war, it had manufactured over two thousand Dive Bombers, Torpedo Bombers and Hawker Hurricanes. The Port Arthur Shipyards, which had not produced anything nautical since 1929, were called upon to produce warships for the Royal Canadian Navy, as fast as they could be turned out. By the end of the war, the shipyards had produced a total of nine Corvettes, six Bangor minesweepers and twenty Algerine minesweepers.

Attracted by work, men and women left the drought of the Prairies and flocked into the Twin Cities to work in the factories, creating a severe housing shortage. Young men from everywhere were being recruited locally into the army, navy and airforce. Airmen from around the Commonwealth learned to fly at the Fort William Airport; sailors trained at HMCS Griffin, the naval barracks; and soldiers were billeted at the Current River Barracks and trained at the Armouries in Port Arthur. Under the auspices of the Children Overseas Reception Board, young evacuees from Britain arrived in Port Arthur to stay for the duration of the war. The "preferred" evacuees, as set down by the Canadian government, were those children unaccompanied by parents or other relatives, medically fit, Anglo-Saxon, non-Roman Catholic, and at least ten years of age.

My friend Kazuo Iwasa recalls that in April 1942, Japanese-Canadian internees were evacuated from British Columbia to Northern Ontario by train under RCMP guard. Dressed only in light clothing they descended into the cold air and scrambled down into a steep ditch to retrieve their duffel bags that had been thrown out of the baggage car. They were interned at an abandoned road camp near Schreiber. Due to the shortage of manpower, they were given the choice of remaining in the camp or harvesting sugar beets in Southern Ontario. Kazuo volunteered to go south. Because of his experience in a British Columbia sawmill, however, he returned to Northern Ontario to work in the area's lumber trade. "There was a great deal of anti-Japanese prejudice in the Lakehead," he recalls, "and the only people who befriended us were the Italians in the Fort William East end. I had my first spaghetti dinner in 1943."

The Japanese and Italian Canadians had much in common. On September 3, 1939 the Government of Canada had issued the Defence of Canada Regulations that created an "enemy alien" class which included not only foreign nationals but also many Canadian citizens. Within two days of Italy's entering the war on the side of Germany in June, 1940, the Canadian government decided an Italian espionage ring was operating in the country and arrested and interned more than seven hundred Italian Canadians, without even the semblance of a hearing. Many spent the war years at Camp Petawawa near Ottawa. Although some had been active Fascists, most had not. From what I can find out, there were few Italians at the Lakehead who belonged to a Fascist party, although a number were Fascist sympathizers. But this sympathy apparently expressed itself in nothing more dangerous than reciting Schiller and Dante, listening to Mussolini's speeches on short-wave radio, or reading *Il Progresso Italo-Americano*, a newspaper published in New York.

Until 1935 when Italy's invasion of Ethiopia turned Britain, and hence Canada, against Italy, one could quite openly and respectably admire Mussolini. The admiration stemmed largely from pride that Italy under *Il Duce* was getting respect from the rest of the world. The international press had lavished praise upon him for his achievements in helping put Italy back on its feet. This, plus *Il Duce's* identification with ancient Rome, could not help but restore a sense of honour to Italian heritage. Il Duce was so popular at the time that his name was featured in a 1934 hit tune by Cole Porter: "You're the top — You're Muss-o-li-ni."

As I remember it, my parents were not particularly interested in Mussolini. When other Italian Canadian women sent their gold wedding bands and jewellery to Mussolini to support his invasion of Ethiopia, Mamma did not.

After Italy's entrance into the war, Canadians of Italian origin were targets of suspicion not only in the government's eyes but in their neighbours'. In a number of cases the RCMP ransacked homes, stores, offices and factories owned by Italian Canadians. They searched for subversive material and concealed weapons. They confiscated and burned Italian language books. Italians without naturalization papers were particularly vulnerable. Luisa S. recalls her experience when her husband John lost his job as a gravedigger:

> I was expecting a second baby. I went to see the Mayor. I told him nobody will give my husband work. Do you want me to steal? I was told, "Watch how you're talking, Lady. They'll put you in the concentration camp." The Mayor asked, "Do you have enough to eat?" I told him I have chickens, pigs. But I don't need food. We want work.

Rita R.'s father was a naturalized Canadian. He owned a shoe repair shop. She was too young to remember when her father was interned. But she does recall that she kept asking her mom, "Where's Daddy?" — and all her mom would say was that Daddy has gone to make shoes for the soldiers.

Debbi M.'s father was also naturalized. He had his own grocery store. All of his children were born and raised in Port Arthur. She told me:

> We came home from school one day and my father was not in the store. He had disappeared all of a sudden. My mother had no idea where he was taken and why. We kids were all young. And so she had to close the store. We had to move. People were throwing stuff at the store windows and we had to take a lot of abuse from our Swedish neighbours. We were called names. We had to go on welfare. We didn't want to, but kids have to be fed.

Shortly after his father's release from the internment camp in 1943, Ted, Debbi's brother, was old enough to join the Navy, and did. He remembers asking his father what it was like in the camp. His father replied, "I couldn't get along with the Germans." That's all he said.

Carmelita, born and raised in Cochrane, was a young woman when her father was interned. She has vivid recollections:

Dad was very proud of being Canadian. He had two sons in the Armed Forces. One played on the Army hockey team in Ottawa — for the Ottawa Commandos. He was an officer.

One night after dinner while Dad was reading, the RCMP just came and grabbed him. He could not even get his coat. No reasons, no explanations. All they asked was "Where is all your Fascist literature?"

Dad owned a grocery store. He was an importer of Italian foods and prominent in Cochrane. There were no Italian societies at that time and very few Italian families. All he had was Mussolini's picture hanging in the back of the store. It was at least ten years old.

He was sent to an internment camp in Petawawa.

I left my job in Timmins and went back to Cochrane to look after the store. Government men went over the books. We hired a lawyer and began writing letters to the Minister of Justice. We badgered the hell out of them. It took six months when Dad finally was let out. He was in the camp seven or eight months. He was sixty-nine years old and naturalized. Within two years he was dead.

It broke my father's heart. They broke him down; they broke his heart. They killed my father who was so gentle and caring. His sons were shattered and devastated too.

The details were always the same: the cloak and dagger surveillance, the sudden raid, the man-handling, the intimidation of the bewildered family, the arrest without warrant and the disappearance of the father. The whole operation was handled in utter secrecy. Government policy was as misguided for the Italians as for the Japanese. Not one of the Italian internees was ever charged with any act of treason or sabotage.

Many Italians were betrayed by their own countrymen during police interrogations and many arrests depended solely on information given by Italian informants. If my parents knew about the arrests and internments, they did not discuss them even in the privacy of our home. Fear undoubtedly prompted silence. Nothing was ever said at Church, at home, or in public that I can remember. There was no press coverage. The whole affair was kept secret on the grounds that exposure would endanger national security.

Despite the injustices of government policy, responses to it varied across Canada. Daddy's treatment was mild. Although he was a naturalized citizen, he, too, had been labelled an "enemy alien." He had been photographed, fingerprinted and interrogated. Every month he had to report to the RCMP headquarters in Fort William. Fortunately, several of the RCMP officers had worked for him, and after a time — I can't remember how long — Daddy no longer had to report to them. He had accepted the

the inconvenience as his patriotic duty. Not once did I hear him complain.

Mamma was just as loyal. Like many Canadian women, Mamma boarded several sailors during the war. And for several months in 1944 she housed a Vancouver Navy officer's wife and young child when they were stranded in Port Arthur without a place to stay. I remember the woman especially well. She was English. She wore pure silk, flesh-coloured stockings. In imitation, I learned to eat grapefruit for breakfast and love it to this day.

Naturally, my parents were worried about their relatives in Italy. Except for his sister Virginia, all of Daddy's family was there. We didn't find out until after the war that our aunt and cousins in Rome had to flee into the mountains and live in caves. And it was only in 1945 when a bank draft Daddy had sent his mother was returned that we discovered she had died in 1944.

In June 1941, at fifteen and a half, Alfred graduated from the Port Arthur Technical and Commercial High School and got a job with the Tomlinson Construction Company. In 1942, the Company sent him to work as bookkeeper in the airport construction jobs at Smithers, Fort St. John, and Prince Rupert in British Columbia. In the Spring of 1943 he joined the Navy at Prince Rupert and was posted to Port Arthur. Because of his speed and quick reflexes, Alfred excelled at all types of sport. Although he was an Ordinary Seaman, he was the acting Physical

Training Instructor for two months in Port Arthur. I used to watch him leading a platoon of sailors running down our street. He was later sent to Cornwallis, N.S. to train as an anti-submarine detector. He served on the Newfie-Derry run in the North Atlantic on the corvette *Halifax* and the frigate *Eastview*. He volunteered for Pacific duty and sailed through the Panama Canal to Comox, B.C., to await his posting when the Atomic Bomb ended the war.

As soon as he was eighteen, Franki, too, joined up, with the Princess Patricia Light Infantry. He was sent to Estevan, Saskatchewan, but was in the service only a few months when peace was declared.

I was so patriotic that I hardly heard the nasty jokes and the belittling slurs, "wop," "dago," "enemy alien." I took Red Cross courses in Home Nursing and First Aid. Luxuries were in short supply, and like other girls I painted my legs with a copper-coloured solution to make them look as if I were wearing stockings. Many pencilled the seams. Since I always had trouble getting the seam straight, I went seamless. And, like other girls, I wrote letters to servicemen on thin blue paper. I wanted to join up. I saw myself as a Wren, even though it was rumoured that only the "tough" girls and the "streetwalkers" enlisted.

I was caught up in the propaganda of war. I hated Hitler and the Germans. I hated Mussolini for being on their side. Proudly I sang, "We're going to hang out our washing on the Siegfried Line, if the Siegfried Line's still there." And we sang "Der Fuehrer's Face":

Ven Der Fuehrer says, Ve iss der Master Race,
Ve Heil Heil Right in Der Fuehrer's Face.

I was so indoctrinated with images of cold-faced goose-stepping German soldiers killing "our boys" that I shall never forget the shock I experienced years later on the first Sunday that I spent in Germany. At a popular restaurant in the Drachenfels ruins, I actually saw Germans making merry. They were eating and drinking and singing their beer songs. I stared at them in disbelief. I had never associated Germans with anything but war.

If Churchill's woeful "I have nothing to offer but blood, toil, tears, and sweat" impressed me with the grim realities of war, Roosevelt's "We have nothing to fear but fear itself" filled me with hope.

In 1942 I graduated from North Bay Normal school. I was a teacher. I got a job at S.S. Number 7 McIntyre, the Onion Lake Road School. My yearly salary was 900 dollars. Daddy agreed to drive me to school before he went to work every morning. I would have to walk the seven miles back home.

The Onion Lake Road School was a one-teacher, one-room frame schoolhouse. Eight classes were crammed into the single room. The ages, sizes and rates of progress of the pupils varied considerably. There were no indoor toilets. I was too shy to use the out-house for fear of being seen by my students. We had no gymnasium, no playground equipment and no art supplies. But I did have my dependable jelly pad (hectograph). I improvised, and the Italian art of *arrangiarsi* stood me in good stead. There were several Finnish and Ukrainian students in Grade 1 who could speak no English. Laura K. remembers that she knew only two English words, "shut up" and "shit." The students were highly motivated, and I was eager to teach them. I wanted to be a good teacher. I wanted to do better than my own teachers had done.

I encouraged an animated patriotic spirit in my little one-room schoolhouse. I tried to impress on the young minds that freedom and justice — the foundation of civilized society — were very much endangered. I enrolled the school in the Junior Red Cross program. And we worked like beavers. We conducted scrap drives for fats, bones, bottles, rags and metal, for the local Salvage Committee. We filled "ditty bags" with chocolate bars, toothpaste, cigarettes, candy, razor blades and shaving soap to send overseas. We knitted socks and a wool afghan 81 in. x 52 in.. I recall that Arthur Johnson, a Grade III student, pledged to buy one twenty-five cents war saving stamp per week. He would bring his nickels to class to exchange for the stamps which I would stick in his booklet for post-war redemption.

In the English literature classes I made the senior students memorize patriotic verses by Kipling. The last stanza from "For All We Have and Are" still comes to mind:

No easy hopes or lies
Shall bring us to our goal,
But iron sacrifice
Of body, will and soul.
There is but one task for all -
One life for each to give.
Who stands if Freedom fall?
Who dies if England live?

Today these lines would be considered jingoistic, but at the time I found them inspiring. Casualty lists filled the newspapers. In one day, August 19, 1942, in the Allied Raid on Dieppe, 3367 of the 5000 Canadians participating were killed, wounded or captured. We remembered them. We honoured them by memorizing John McCrae's "In Flanders Fields" and Lawrence Binyon's "For the Fallen":

They shall not grow old, as we that are left
* grow old:*
Age shall not weary them, nor the years con-
* demn.*
At the going down of the sun and in the
* morning*
We will remember them.

Yvonne O. remembers that I taught popular war songs, such as "This Is the Army,

Mr. Jones" and "What Do You Do in the Infantry?" The senior girls liked to sing "There'll Always Be an England" and the Vera Lynn classic, "There'll Be Bluebirds Over the White Cliffs of Dover."

At sixteen years of age Yvonne was a special student, older than the others and only two years younger than I was. She had missed several years of school because she was needed at home. She became my Girl Friday. I was responsible for hot lunches, but knew nothing about cooking, so it was Yvonne who made moose meat stew and hot cocoa. She was also the school janitor and was paid sixteen dollars a month, money her family used to buy feed for the farm animals. I recall that the school was poorly heated and I taught in a snowsuit all winter long. To this day Yvonne remembers how purple my fingers would get.

Occasionally, I was able to hitch a ride home with a passing dump-truck. Because of gas-rationing, there were virtually no cars on the road. In November and December my hands, even with mitts on, got so numb that Mamma would have a basin of warm water ready for me. Oh, how my hands would sting!

Boarding houses for teachers were difficult to find. But from January to April I was able to board with a Ukrainian couple who lived a mile from the school. They spoke no English but had great respect for teachers. The wife made her husband sleep on a couch so that I would be more comfortable sleeping with her in the only bed in the house. In bed I held myself at the edge of the mattress, against the wall, so as not to touch her. It was bitterly cold, and I never got up during the night. The only facility was a pail on the porch. I did not like the arrangement but there was no alternative.

At the end of the year, my school inspector, W.J.J., recommended me for Five Mile School on the Dawson Road, which had nearly fifty students and all eight grades. I considered myself a lucky girl. The larger, one-room school would be a welcome opportunity to do greater things. I got more money too. I think it was one hundred and ten dollars a month. I still paid Mamma thirty dollars a month room and board. And I had money left over to buy my first book-case, and then books from a travelling salesman. I was thrilled with these purchases. But in buying the books — a set of four volumes by Mark Twain and another set of three by Louis Bromfield — I had unknowingly committed myself to a two-year subscription for several magazines whose names escape me now. How I resented having to pay for magazines I did not want! However, the experience taught me to be wary of door-to-door salesmen. I also bought a black raccoon coat. It was my first fur coat. War time regulations limited the length of women's fur coats. Nevertheless my short fur coat kept me warm, and it looked great.

And I bought lots of sheet music. By this time my ten years of music studies were paying off. I had passed the theoretical and practical exams as required by the University of Toronto and in 1942 I was awarded their ATCM degree in pianoforte as a Solo Performer. I had struggled with timidity and prejudice to compete in festivals. I had been the organist at St. Anthony's Church. I was honoured by the Thunder Bay branch of the Canadian Federation of University Women who invited me, as a recipient of their Grade XIII award, to play the piano at their monthly meeting which was held in the splendid Norman Room of the Royal Edward Hotel in Fort William. When the President and Secretary called to pick me up at home, I did not even stop to introduce them to Mamma because I was ashamed of her broken English. For the occasion, I wore a chocolate brown silk dress with gold piping around the dropped waist and Peter Pan collar. I played Brahms's "Capriccio in B minor." The women were delighted. I played an encore, David W. Guion's "The Harmonica Player." I was very pleased until Miss Belle E. took me aside and confided, "Never wear brown, Serafina. It's not your colour." I never made that mistake again.

I was able to bring my musical enthusiasm and expertise to my teaching. In fact, I was so devoted to music that I had not taken the job at Onion Lake Road School until the board bought a piano. A second-hand one was all they could afford. But I was pleased.

At the Five Mile School my Christmas Concert of 1943 was a hit. In those days the Christmas Concert was the most important annual event for a rural community, which judged a teacher's worth by its success or failure. We had practised hard at noon hours, at recesses, and after four for over a month. I was a Sergeant-Major. I drilled and drilled until my students had perfected their routines, recitations, songs and skits. I played the piano, conducted, choreographed, directed and prompted. The little kids acted out "The Dwarf's Marching Song" from *Snow White*. They sang "Christmas Cavalcade" and "Swinging on a Star" from *Going my Way*. The older ones danced *Comin' Through the Rye, The Sailor's Hornpipe*, and the *Hop-Scotch Polka*. The senior girls sang the descant to "Silent Night." And everybody sang "Hark the Herald Angels Sing." For a moment the war was forgotten.

The musical event that stands out clearly in my memory is the piano recital my colleague and I gave for our A.T.C.M. degrees on June 30, 1944. I had asked my inspector permission to dismiss school an hour early that day. He refused, and so I taught until four o'clock. The recital was to begin at eight. My music teacher had told me that it was common practice to be presented with a bouquet of flowers after each stage appearance — flowers that would be sent by friends. I replied that I couldn't ask anybody to send me flowers. At home I mentioned my fears that there wouldn't be any for me. We hadn't even invited anybody. Mamma and I did not want to impose on anyone. Besides, flowers were such an indulgence.

On the evening of the recital, bouquets kept arriving for my colleague. Nothing for me. My heart sank. Finally, a dozen red roses came from my sister Rita's boss, the manager of the Port Arthur Café where she worked part-time. And a half-dozen from Mamma's friend, Chichina G., a generous and progressive Italian woman. I breathed a sigh of relief. But I would be making four stage appearances. I didn't know what was going to happen. To this day I don't know how I survived the evening. I know that my playing disappointed my teacher. And I was ashamed. As for the flowers, I was presented with the same bunch several times.

In those days St. Anthony's Church did not offer any social activities for its young people. I had often wished that it had a CGIT like St. Paul's United where my neighbour Ann went to church. But St. Anthony's pastor was not the Father O'Malley of *Going My Way*. Although St. Andrew's Church, where the rich Catholics went, had a young people's group, it was cliquish, and the few times that I went I felt like an outsider.

And yet life in World War II Port Arthur was exciting. I was caught up in the glamour and romance of war on the homefront. There was the gala atmosphere of Victory Loan parades, military bands and marching men. There were soldiers, sailors and airmen to meet. There were rousing send-offs for the Lake Superior Regiment which left for overseas service on October 10, 1940, and for the Algonquin Regiment which left Port Arthur on June 4, 1941. There were ships in the harbour to visit. There were public dances.

With my ethnic girlfriends, all of whom had gone to the Tech, "my cohorts" I called them, I would go to a café — the Main, the Port Arthur, or the Twin City — and sit until late at night sipping five-cent cokes and listening to the hit tunes from the juke box in our booth: "Tangerine" by the Tommy Dorsey Orchestra, Benny Goodman's "And the Angels Sing," or Vaughan Munroe's "There I've Said it Again." The Andrew Sisters and Frank Sinatra were our favourite singers, followed closely by Bing Crosby, Dinah Shore and Nat King Cole. We loved to sing along with tunes, such as "You are My Sunshine," "Ma, He's Kissing Me" or "Oh, Johnny, Oh Johnny, How You Can Love." Harry James playing "You Made Me Love You" on his trumpet kept us spellbound, as did Glenn Miller's swing trombone.

I still remember the fun we would have on our way home, singing songs like "Praise the Lord and Pass the Ammunition" or "Kiss Me Goodnight Sergeant-Major."

Dancing was my obsession. Two or three times a week I went with my cohorts to our favourite places — the *Finn Hall*, the *SOE Hall*, or the *Legion* — to dance to the music of the Lakehead's big bands: Stan Onski, Ted Goodsell, Hugh Paxton and Joe Turner. I loved dancing to "Begin the Beguine," "Stormy Weather" or "Siboney," which Xavier Cugat made famous. But most of all I loved to jitterbug to "The Dark Town Strutter's Ball" and "In the Mood." And I never sat out "Buttons and Bows," "Don't Fence Me In" or "Pistol Packin Mamma."

We went unescorted. Men were plentiful, and we were asked to dance every number, which gave us a sense of power. Sailors especially had a mysterious appeal for us. We never refused them a dance.

However, we were very careful whom we allowed to take us out for a coke or to walk us home. Pacts that we would not separate had to be kept. There was safety in numbers. Society categorized women into two groups. Those who "would" were the bad girls and those who "wouldn't" were the good girls. We had our reputations to protect. We were not out for "hanky-panky." We did not smoke or drink. I once charmed an Algonquin out of his regimental badge and wore it on the waistband of my slacks; I once teased an airman out of his wings and sewed them high on the left sleeve of my new powder-blue coat. But these were only tests of my charms.

I went to scores of dances but only two are etched in memory. One was an occasion on which several sailors invited my girlfriends and me to a dance at the Naval Barracks. After a short time we were asked to leave because it was a *hostess* dance (all the girls present were specially invited). I was mortified because a few of my PACI classmates had noticed me.

On another occasion, I was at the elegant ballroom of the Royal Edward Hotel in Fort William. I was dancing when suddenly my "step-ins" fell on the floor. (During the war, panties — step-ins — were held together on the side with little pearl buttons because there was no elastic for domestic use). I was terribly embarrassed as I stepped out of my undies and hastened to the washroom.

No matter how prudish I was, Mamma still did not approve of my going out on dates. All servicemen were "soldiers" to Mamma. They were "birds of passage" — here today, gone tomorrow — never to be trusted. The opposite sex had only one thing in mind. And I believed it truly.

In those days sex was such a forbidden topic that my girlfriends and I would have felt shame and guilt if we had ever talked "dirty." Mamma did not know the English word for sex, and I do not know whether there is a Calabrese equivalent.

In a Calabrese home, the names of the shameful body parts were never mentioned. There was never any display of conjugal affection, and the word "love" was never used. Nakedness and talk of body functions were taboo. We received no instruction as to how babies were made or where they came from.

One day when I was kneeling down on the floor reciting the *Angelus* in a classroom at St. Joseph's Academy, I felt a trickle of something going down my legs. In the washroom I was horrified at the sight. God must be punishing me for something evil that I had done. I kept my guilt a secret. Then, like a thunderbolt, the thought came to me that Mamma must have had the same thing happen to her. I remembered the pails of bloody water and the large white napkins hanging on the line. I knew where she kept her napkins in her chest of drawers. I took a few. For two years I snitched her napkins and attached them to my panties with large safety pins. Whether she ever missed them, I do not know. Later, I discovered that this monthly happening was called "the curse." But why it occurred and what it meant, I only learned much later, in bits and pieces.

Mamma's idea of a sexual education was summed up in one warning when I was leaving to go to Teachers' College — a sweep of her arm across her abdomen which I understood to mean "Don't expect to come home if you get yourself in trouble." Premarital chastity was sacrosanct. Preserving one's virginity was a religious duty. Sex was dangerous.

I had all sorts of hang-ups, even drawing back from the occasional chaste kiss. I wondered what the "French kiss" was like. But even that curiosity made me feel guilty. Young men told me that Italian girls were supposed to be "passionate." I was an "iceberg." I was scared to death if a boy's hands began to wander. When I was nineteen, three girlfriends and I were hitchhiking and were picked up by a young man who wanted to impress us. He started to drive too fast. I was so fearful of jeopardizing my virginity that I took no chances and jumped out of the speeding car. I never told Mamma.

And yet I did all sorts of things which Italian girls were traditionally forbidden to do. I wore makeup and painted my fingernails and toenails. I went swimming at a public pool in Current River Park. I went to public dances. Mary drove me on her bike, side saddle, to Boulevard Lake. I drove a car. I could smoke and drink if I wanted.

Although I accused Mamma of being "old-fashioned," she was, as I think back to-day, ahead of her time. Canada was changing her. There has always been the tendency in Calabrese culture to dote on sons, but I never felt that Mamma did this. Nor did she put pressure on her girls to get married. I doubt that she approved of the conventional *ambasciata* (informal overture to an arranged marriage). And she never expected me to participate in the *passaggiata*, a ritual wereby young women displayed themselves by strolling up and down the street, locked arm in arm, as they did, traditionally, in Southern Italy. I did not have a hope chest to fill. I did not have my ears pierced. I did not turn my pay cheque over to her. She made me my first pair of slacks. A friend told me recently how envious she was when she saw me in my slacks because her mother would not allow her to wear "pants." I appeared in bathing suits at Boulevard Lake despite Mamma's disapproval of my "parading" in such scanty clothing.

The feminist revolution was decades away and girls still conformed exclusively to the image of beauty as defined by a male dominated society and women's magazines. Men focused obsessively on good looks. We looked to the sleek and sexy Hollywood pin-up girls as our models of beauty: Gene Tierney, Rita Hayworth, Carole Lombard and Lana Turner. I always wished for a "peaches and cream" complexion and blonde hair that I could wear like Veronica Lake's smooth golden tresses, falling provocatively over one eye.

I was anxious about my looks — saw myself with a mixture of pleasure and dread. My friend Helvi applied makeup to camouflage my pimples. She was an expert in making the most of my features. She spread cold cream over my face with her fingers. Then she dabbed on powder with a puff. She smoothed rouge on my cheek bones. She brushed mascara on my eyelashes and curled them. She dabbed green eyeshadow on my lids. All the while we laughed and chanted, "She's engaged. She's lovely. She uses Pond's."

I learned the hard way that the popular rhyme "Guys don't make passes at girls who wear glasses" was true. I did not want guys who made passes, but I did want to be noticed. I tried an experiment in the summer of 1943. I went to a public dance wearing my glasses. I was not asked for a single dance. The next night I did not wear them. Thirty men asked me to dance. I refused each one. Even though it meant trying to function with blurred vision, I never went to another dance wearing my glasses. Ten years later when contact lenses became avalaible in Port Arthur, I bought a pair immediately. They were not the contemporary soft lenses, but were made of hard glass and covered the whole eye. I could barely tolerate them. Through the years of discomfort and pain to come, I would keep repeating Mamma's Calabrese proverb, "No pain, no gain." I knew my eyes were my best feature and I wanted to emphasize them. They were hazel but would turn green when I wore my contacts. I can still recall the time when I entered the Officers' Mess at #2 Fighter Wing in France where I was teaching, and the piano player announced that he was playing "She has the eyes of a woman in love," for me. Oh, what a difference my contacts made to my self-confidence!

But my real pride was in my figure. I tried to keep it firm and slender. I ate sparingly and avoided fats. I also wore a girdle — a "must" in those days — which gave my figure a smooth line. When I walked down the street, young men whistled. I enjoyed it, but I pretended not to notice. By this time I had learned how to dress. It was difficult to find dresses in the colours that best suited me: white, red, yellow, and pink. And so I spent hours finding fabrics of the right colours and getting fitted at my dressmaker's. I could wear a knitted suit.

Despite my beautiful clothes, the makeup, and name change, I still suffered negative feelings about myself. I was self-conscious about my acne, my thick eyeglasses and my *Italianness*.

Luckily I could teach. When my superiors expressed admiration for my mind, I felt vindicated.

And I also did get the occasional boost to my self-esteem. Once at a dance at Wonderland, in London, Ontario, where I was taking courses at the University of Western Ontario during the summer of 1944, I was told that I looked like Elizabeth Taylor. Because I did not frequent the movies (I was protecting my eyesight), the comparison did not mean anything at the time. I soon discovered its implications, however, and was, needless to say, flattered.

I got another morale booster when the Ottawa Women's Voluntary Service introduced the idea of using "attractive" young women as "Miss Canada" girls to advertise the national sale of War Savings stamps. I dared to volunteer, and, to my surprise I was one of twelve Port Arthur girls selected. I was sent to busy downtown street corners and baseball games to sell stamps. I exuded a youthful exuberance. I had style. I hustled and sold a lot of stamps. I was so proud to be helping my country. I loved being seen in my uniform: a red wedge cap and a red apron with "Miss Canada" emblazoned across it in bold white letters.

And yet I suspected somehow that I was the foot-soldier, slogging it out on pavement and field. But I was too afraid to ask — let alone, to complain. (It wasn't until I began searching for photos for this book that I discovered that my suspicions had been well-founded. There had been a clique, an in-group, who were invited to a number of civic galas; who had participated in a movie that the National Film Board made of the launching of the Corvette, *Port Arthur*, and who had been invited to a première showing of the movie, and the launching of the algerine *H.M.C.S. Wallaceburg*.)

All the while I was trying to straddle two worlds in a tug-of-war between the home and the "outside," between Mamma and me. In the traditional Southern Italian family, obedience to parental authority, regardless of age, was absolute. As long as we were little children, obedient and submissive, Mamma was able to keep a tightly knit family circle — "circus" as she pronounced it. Good children thought first of their parents and then themselves. The well-being of the family was put above individual indulgence and personal mobility. But the more individualistic we became, the more we disrupted the solidarity of *la famiglia*. Family solidarity, as Mamma had known it in her *paesello* in Calabria, provided a power that superseded that of any institution in the country.

Loyalties outside the home impinged on family solidarity. *Stranieri* (strangers) were to be avoided. They would invariably let you down. Time and again Mamma repeated the phrases that governed her Old World life: "*Non dare confidenza*" (Don't take anybody into your confidence); "*Non ti fidare di nessuno*" (Trust no one). They are still fresh in my memory.

Slowly Mamma's family disintegrated around her. We no longer spoke the same language. There were no Calabrese equivalents for *dating, rights, fulfilment, identity*. Our family functioned with few words.

And yet Mamma still tried to control my behaviour. Year after year she flung her pithy aphorisms of Calabrese folk wisdom: "*Chi ti vo male ti fa rirere*" (People who wish you evil make you laugh); "*Chi ti vo bene ti fa chiangere*" (People who wish you well make you cry); "*E meglio stare sula che male accompagnata*" (Better to be alone than with the wrong company); "*Chine te vo bene ciu di mamma o ti trade o t'inganna*" (Whoever wishes you well more than your mother either betrays you or tricks you).

I steadfastly asserted my individuality. It was hard to be a dutiful Calabrese daughter and a young Canadian at the same time. In later years I travelled to strange countries around the globe. Mamma's constant refrain was: "*U pede che assai anna ciu presto perde che guadagna*" (The foot that wanders too much loses more than it gains). Her last words each time I left home would haunt me: "Go away but you won't find me here when you come back."

An incident during the Winter of 1943 struck deep into my youthful consciousness. A girlfriend and I went to a house party on Ontario Street, a block away from our house. I had not told Mamma I was going. When I was not home by midnight she decided to go outside to look for me. To this day I do not know how she found me — she told me she followed footprints in the newly-fallen snow. The party was going full swing when I was told my mother was at the door. She made me put on my coat and silently escorted me out of the house.

But I kept insisting on my personal freedom, and eventually Mamma resigned herself to the inevitable. She consoled herself with her own Calabrese proverbs: "*Figli e mariti come Dio ti le manda*" (Children and husbands as God sends them to you).

At times she would invoke the Holy Spirit to "illuminate" me: "*U Santo Spiritu t'alumma.* Or she would say "*Dio te benedica*" and entrust me into God's care.

12
Epilogue

It is now half a century later. I have travelled around the world. I've been to England and Calabria. I have been teaching most of my life. I taught in Germany, France and Uganda. I've lectured in a number of Italian universities. I now live on the top of the hill overlooking Secord Street where I grew up.

In the Autumn of 1963 when I was teaching in Africa, I received a call telling me that Daddy was seriously ill. I left Africa immediately. On the long flight home, memories of a physical strength and courage that had tamed the Northern wilderness came to mind. Memories of Daddy's capricious temper came too.

When I saw him in his hospital bed, he seemed so frail, helpless, gentle. He wept to see me. I forgot all my hurts. The last time I saw him he blessed me and called me his "first flower." He died two weeks later.

Even though Daddy had often said in jest that the northern weather could be summed up as ten months of winter and two months of hard sledding, he loved the North. He loved the land: its rocks, its pines and clear cold waters.

After Daddy died, Mamma often spoke of going back to Piane Crati. She could never forget the *paesello* of her youth. And she looked back with longing and lost values. Although she had become enamoured of the British monarchy and was interested in Canadian politics, she identified with the great persons of Italian history, art, music, exploration and invention.

In November 1947, at a banquet honouring the Italian-Canadian veterans of World War II, Mamma, as President of the Italian Ladies' Society of Port Arthur, had referred to the men as *"buoni figlioli italiani"* (good sons of Italy) and *"buoni cittadini canadesi"* (good citizens of Canada). She referred to herself as *"una madre pattriotica."*

Mamma bore the loneliness of her final years with quiet dignity. I can still see her in the La-z-Boy chair, in front of the corner shrine where she kept an assortment of holy pictures. Hour by hour she fingered the beads of her Rosary which were held together, in places, by strands of black thread where the tiny links had broken. At times the prayers that had supported her all her life did not seem to give her solace.

Toward the end she was constantly preparing for death. On one occasion she told Father Rizzi which Latin prayers were to be recited at her funeral Mass. The Father replied that he was sorry but he no longer had the Latin prayers. This was post-Vatican II. Mamma, ever resourceful, replied that she could get her prayers copied for him.

Another time, when she was in the hospital, she asked for a priest to administer Extreme Unction. She was making sure that she was going to have "the grace of a happy death." The hospital called me and I hurried over with my friend Jim. When we arrived, the priest was trying to read the last rites, but he had forgotten his glasses and could not see the print in his book. Jim offered the priest his glasses. But the priest could barely see out of them. He made an error. Mamma, who until that point was "near death" sprang up in bed and corrected him.

Mamma died in January 1979. She left a hand-written note in her phonetic English, instructing us as to how she wanted to be laid out, and in what clothes. All her life she had prided herself on her solidly corseted figure. The Spirella corsetiere had come to the house and measured her for the correct fit. With its metal staves and two sets of laces at the back and front, her corset took some time to fasten, but she had never come down stairs in the morning without it on. I brought Mamma's clothes, including the corset, to the funeral home. The director followed her instructions. But when I saw Mamma in her casket, her stiffened body looked so unnatural that I had the director remove the corset.

Education, which Mamma had promoted so passionately, enabled her children entrance into the professional and business worlds, unachievable goals in her day in Calabria. But that closely knit family circle, rooted so deeply in her Calabrese psyche, had eluded her. The myth of America had promised economic gain, not happiness. We were her America. She accepted her destiny and the destinies of her offspring as the will of God, a fate beyond her control.

Acknowledgements

I should like to thank the following people who, in so many ways, have been helpful to me in the preparation of my manuscript by sharing memories or giving me hospitality, information, photographs and moral support: Fanny Albanese, Dora and Roy Alto, Donald Bliss, Nikki Burns, Theresa Cava, Theresa Chocla, Vi D'Agostino, Celestino DeIulius, Rose and John Elia, Furine Foley, Flavio and Willie Ferris, Edith Gagliardi, Annina Garofolo, Rita Covello Gravina, Debbi Hacio, James Isbester, Kaz Iwasa, Laura Koivo, Helvi Kotanen, Rita Kubinek, Lawrence and Rita McCall, Verna McKercher, Angus McLean, Ted Maltese, Ida Mauro, Norma Mortellaro, Rita Nevins, Yvonne Olenik, Alfred, Leonardo, Maria, Mary, Michael and Natalina Petrone, Mario Piano, Rita Pradissitto, Edith Prezio, Vilma Ricci, Maria Rigato, Gina Rimanich, June Seabrook, Madeline Sisco, Helen Sjonnsen, Luisa Soldera, Carlo Sprovieri, Armand Talarico, Tory Tronrud and Nella Vaacher.

I should like to mention the Reference Departments of Waverley and Brodie Resource

Libraries and of Lakehead University Library for their constant co-operation.

I am also grateful to Joan Skelton who commented on my preliminary draft, and asked, "Where is my Penny?"; to Sylvia Bowerbank who made invaluable suggestions, and to Charles Wilkins for his help.

And special thanks go to the Senate Research Committe of Lakehead University for their financial assistance.

(Note: Throughout this book, the Calabrese dialect was favoured to formal Italian.)

List of Photographs

Chapter One: *Gli Americani*; Daddy (centre) and friends.
Chapter Two: The Waterfront (c. 1910); Mamma and Daddy's wedding party.
Chapter Three: Mamma (on the left) loved to be well dressed; Mamma dancing the Tarantella.
Chapter Four: *U bosso; U mareschiallo*.
Chapter Five: South End Gang; The Prezio and Petrone families with Nanna (c. 1930).
Chapter Six: Alfred; Franki.
Chapter Seven: The three little sisters; Mamma and Daddy's Silver Anniversary.
Chapter Eight: St. Anthony's Church; Main Altar.
Chapter Nine: Penny's Grade 8 class at St. Joseph's; Penny at ten; Penny in a bathing suit; Penny as Miss Canada.
Chapter Ten: P.A.C.I.; Daddy's Ford V-8.
Chapter Eleven: Recital.
Epilogue: Penny and Rita at Fort Lauderdale, Florida.

- Cap-Saint-Ignace
- Sainte-Marie (Beauce)
  Québec, Canada
  1995